THE PHILOSOPHY OF CLASSICAL YOGA

THE PHILOSOPHY OF CLASSICAL YOGA

GEORG FEUERSTEIN

Inner Traditions International
Rochester, Vermont

Inner Traditions International
One Park Street
Rochester, Vermont 05767

LIBRARY OF CONGRESS CATALOGING-IN-PUBLICATION DATA
Feuerstein, Georg
The philosophy of classical yoga / Georg Feuerstein.
p. cm.
Originally published: New York : St. Martin's Press, 1980.
Includes bibliographical references and index.
ISBN 0-89281-603-1
1. Yoga. I. Title.
B132.Y6F47 1996
181'.45–dc20 96–14380
CIP
Printed and bound in Canada

10 9 8 7 6 5 4 3 2 1

Distributed to the book trade in Canada by Publishers Group West (PGW), Toronto, Ontario

Distributed to the book trade in the United Kingdom by Deep Books, London

Distributed to the book trade in Australia by Millennium Books, Newtown, N. S. W.

Distributed to the book trade in New Zealand by Tandem Press, Auckland

Distributed to the book trade in South Africa by Alternative Books, Randburg

Contents

Foreword

by Professor Corrado Pensa

The study of oriental philosophical-religious texts, especially of the Indian genre, presents considerable and particular difficulties. In many instances there is a lack of adequate historical and chronological data, and frequently all that remains are the name of the author and a few vague and more or less legendary reports about him. Furthermore, the terms which confront one are so polyvalent and stratified as to constitute often a very real challenge to anyone who seeks to gauge their full meaning.

In the face of all these difficulties it is of primary importance to develop a valid methodology in order to determine the parameters necessary for the most correct interpretation of eastern texts. It gives me, therefore, great pleasure to preface this book by Georg Feuerstein, who has been researching into Yoga for many years with investigative passion and has already given us several works of capital importance for the comprehension of this subject. His previous books *A Reappraisal of Yoga*, *The Essence of Yoga* and *Textbook of Yoga* testify to an increasing appreciation of Yoga, which is considered each time from a different angle, always enriching our understanding of this phenomenon.

In his methodology Feuerstein adopts an approach to research in which accurate linguistic analysis is inseparable from the analysis of the various contexts in which a given term or concept appears, thus ensuring that all possible meaning values are identified. This particular question has been treated in some depth in the companion volume to the present work entitled *Yoga-Sūtra: An Exercise in the Methodology of Textual Analysis*.

The central premise of this methodology is the rejection of all simplistic unilateral interpretations. For this reason Feuerstein also correctly criticises in the aforementioned work E. Conze's reduction of Yoga to a mere assemblage of techniques, whereas what we are in fact dealing with is a 'theory–practice continuum'. Hence, again, his refusal to blindly trust the interpretational keys proffered in the exegetical Sanskrit literature postdating the *Yoga-Sūtra*; as he points out there is a considerable intervening chronological *and* ideological distance. Although taking due note of the commentaries, Feuerstein prefers to concentrate on an immanent critique of the original text itself.

In contrast to the approach adopted by many Orientalists who *a priori* tend to deny the unity of the text under examination, fragmenting it into so many parts or heterogeneous strata until nothing remains, Feuerstein rightly asks in his methodological study whether this compulsive search for incongruencies and textual corruptions is not the expression of an ethnocentric rationalising mentality which inclines to project everywhere its own need for abstract and absolute logic, and hence is particularly prone to misinterpret paradoxical expressions so common in eastern thought, which has a *penchant* for transcending dualism and therefore in part also rational language as such.

The principal merit of the present volume lies in that it provides us with a highly original overall picture of Classical Yoga. Instead of giving a contracted description of this school of thought – which would be at least partly second-hand – Feuerstein undertakes a thorough analysis of the key concepts, arranging his findings in a systematic fashion so that in the end there spontaneously emerges a complete picture of the entire spiritual *iter* of Classical Yoga. His detailed semantic examination demonstrates once again – if that should still be necessary – that the meaning of the complex and polyvalent Sanskrit terms (hardly ever translatable into our languages by a single word) must be sought through an accurate comparison of the various contexts in which they occur.

The other great merit of this work is that it never loses sight of the psycho-integrative and experiential matrix of a great many key concepts of Classical Yoga. Thus *īśvara*, considered by a number of Orientalists as a later superfluous interpolation added from the outside to a system already complete in itself, is here linked up with the *yogin*'s profound experience of the archetypal *yogin*, *i.e.* the macrocosmic reflection of the *puruṣa* innate in everybody, which in its turn is not an abstract concept but a concrete numinous experience whose connections with the conditioned mental complexes (the *punctum dolens* of many exegetes and scholars) are here analysed with considerable precision.

Also with regard to the concept of *prakṛti* the author's observations are stimulating and original, particularly in his recognition of two distinct levels – a 'deep structure' and a 'surface structure', which opens up new lines of research. The same may be said of certain parallels which he draws between the *guṇa* theory and recent discoveries in nuclear physics.

Yoga is here interpreted in terms of a profound transformation of consciousness culminating in *gnosis*. After having shown in his probing study that it is essentially a bi-polar process of gradual internalisation, he reaches a conclusion of enormous significance which, in my opinion, is fundamental to all Indian thought: 'the ontogenetic models are originally and primarily maps for meditative introspection'. This homologisation between cosmological and psychological structures is truly a modality of thought intrinsic to the Indian religious consciousness, as was noted already by M. Falk in her brilliant and unfortunately little known study *Il mito psicologico nell'India antica* (Rome, 1939).

It is to be hoped that works such as Georg Feuerstein's present study will serve as a stimulus so that other scholars may enrich their own methods of research in order to contribute to a more valid and differentiated view of Indian religiosity.

Rome, 1979

Preface

Yoga, in particular Patañjali's variant of this great Indian tradition, has capitivated my professional interest over many years, and my published findings and thoughts on the subject reflect the various stages of this protracted research. The present volume consists of a series of detailed analyses of the key concepts mustered by Patañjali to describe and explain the enigma of human existence and to point a way out of conditioned existence, to stop the perpetual motion of the 'wheel of becoming' (*bhava-cakra* = *saṃsāra*).

I have adopted an historical approach combined with a system-immanent interpretation founded on my own rigorous textual studies on the structure of Patañjali's work, the *Yoga-Sūtra* (see my 1979 methodological study). This book differs from previous publications in that it seeks to wrest from Patañjali's aphoristic statements themselves the philosophical edifice of Classical Yoga and thus to combat the overpowering influence exercised by Vyāsa's scholium, the *Yoga-Bhāṣya*, on all subsequent efforts at exegesis. By contrast, I have tried to tentatively relate Patañjali's conceptions to *earlier* epic teachings from which, after all, he must have drawn some inspiration. In fact, there appears to be a far greater continuity between Classical Yoga and antecedent (pre-classical) formulations than is normally thought. However, the present work does not develop this point further, and the parallels introduced have the chief purpose of illuminating Patañjali's teachings.

There are naturally many details of this intricate *darśana* which, of necessity, had to be relegated to a secondary place, although they could profitably form the substance of further problem-specific studies. My principal aim has been to present a reinterpretation of the main bearings of the metaphysical framework of Classical Yoga. The single most important finding of this piece of research is the fact that Patañjali's system cannot be subsumed under the heading of Sāṃkhya. Classical Yoga is exactly what its protagonists claim: an automomonous *darśana* with its own characteristic set of concepts and technical expressions. The popular scholarly impression according to which Classical Yoga is some kind of parasite, capitalising on the philosophical efforts of Classical Sāṃkhya, is shown to be in need of urgent and radical revision. The concluding chapter is a thumbnail sketch of the crucial differences between these two schools which should set this whole issue into the proper perspective.

Some readers may be puzzled by the sparing treatment afforded to the famous schema of the 'eight members' (*aṣṭa-aṅga*) of Yoga, frequently misinterpreted as 'stages'. The reason for this is twofold. First, I have dealt with this aspect of Classical Yoga fairly extensively in a previous book (see my 1974 publication) and second, I have come to regard this particular systematisation of the yogic path as of subsidiary importance in the overall structure of Patañjali's school of thought. In fact, it is highly probable that he adopted this eightfold classification from earlier sources for the sake of expositional convenience, whereas his own view seems to be that *kriyā-yoga*, which can be equated with Classical Yoga *per se*, is essentially the combined practice of ascesis (*tapas*), self-study (*svādhyāya*) and devotion to the Lord (*īśvara-praṇidhāna*) (see aphorism II.1), which leads to the cultivation of the enstatic consciousness (in *samādhi*) and consequently to the abrogation of those factors which are the true causes of human bondage and man's mistaken self-identity.

The observations, thoughts, suggestions and speculations presented in this fascicle have all matured on the soil prepared by previous researchers, and my criticisms of some of their contributions, though necessarily committed, in no way seek to detract from the merit of their valuable labour. I am particularly indebted to the work of the late Professor J. W. Hauer, which first introduced me to the exciting possibility of a text-immanent interpretation of the *Yoga-Sūtra*. To what degree I have succeeded in achieving this programme, future studies will undoubtedly evince.

Several friends and colleagues have made various contributions at different stages in the writing of this book. My special thanks go to Professor Dr Arnold Kunst and Dr Tuvia Gelblum for their comments; to Professor Corrado Pensa for the generous remarks in his Foreword; to Mr J. H. M. Shankland for Englishing the Italian Foreword; to Mrs Mary Newman for reading through the entire script and righting a number of linguistic wrongs; to Mrs A. Mitchell for tackling so efficiently the typing of a fairly complicated manuscript; to Dr Richard Lawless and the secretaries of the Middle East Documentation Centre (Durham), especially Miss Avril Yeates, for various favours and kindnesses; and not least to the library staff of the School of Oriental Studies (Durham), in particular Dr R. Char and Mr Malcolm Ferguson, for their considerateness and help in procuring seemingly unprocurable works.

June 1979

Preface to the New Edition

I am grateful to Ehud Sperling, publisher of Inner Traditions International, for giving this book a new lease on life, after having been out of print for many years. Its subject matter is as relevant today as it was when I wrote about it sixteen years ago, and I am happy to say that the present work, short as it is, still offers the most systematic, in-depth analysis of the principal concepts of Classical Yoga.

This monograph is complemented by some of my other books, notably *The Yoga-Sutra of Patañjali; A New Translation and Commentary*, also published by Inner Traditions International, and *Wholeness or Transcendence? Ancient Lessons for the Emerging Global Civilization*, published by Larson Publications.

Georg Feuerstein, Ph.D.
Yoga Research Center
P.O. Box 1386
Lower Lake, CA 95457

I

The Concept of God (*īśvara*)

The ontology of Classical Yoga, or *kriyā-yoga*, has three major foci, *viz*. *īśvara*, *puruṣa* and *prakṛti*. These are deemed irreducible ontic ultimates. The most distinctive feature of the ontology of Patañjali's school of thought and, I wish to contend, of any form of hindu Yoga, is the concept of 'the Lord' or *īśvara*.

The word *īśvara* is a derivative of the verbal root $\sqrt{\textit{īś}}$ ('to rule'), current already at the time of the ancient vedic *saṃhitās*. Synonyms are *īś*, *īśa* and *īśana*, *īśvara* being the more prevalent form in later periods. It conveys the notion of a highest personal god, at times endowed with certain anthropomorphic characteristics but never totally divorced from the concept of the impersonal absolute, the *brahman*, of philosophical discourse. The term *īśvara* is ultimately bound up with the history of theism in India.

Repeated attempts have been made in the past to trace the evolution of this crucial religio-philosophical concept. One of the first scholars to apply himself to the study of the history of theism was M. Müller. He distinguished three principal stages, all of which can be evidenced still in the vedic age; they are (1) Polytheism, (2) Henotheism (or Kathenotheism), (3^a) Monotheism and (3^b) Pantheism.

Thus on the most archaic level M. Müller (1916^4) envisaged a kind of theological pluralism in which the thirty-three known gods of the ṛgvedic pantheon were regarded as embodiments or abstractions of natural phenomena. On the basis of this diffuse conceptual stage the need arose for a unification of the multiple *devas* populating the heavens. According to M. Müller, the notion of the *viśve-devas* ('all-gods') was a gambit in this direction. Certain gods were identified with each other or coupled together, as in the case of Mitra-Varuṇa and Agni-Soma, etc. On the next stage, in M. Müller's evolutionary scheme, a single god was invoked under the temporary forgetfulness of all other gods. For this phenomenon he devised the term Henotheism (also: Kathenotheism). From then on the development proceeded in a bifurcate line. On the one hand it gave rise to monotheistic conceptions and on the other hand to Pantheism with its impersonal absolute.

The entire problem was renewedly investigated by H. Jacobi (1923). In principle accepting M. Müller's (1916^4) classificatory model, he modified somewhat his formulation of the nature of Henotheism in that he preferred to regard it not so much as a direct pre-stage to Monotheism, but as a rejection of the gods as totally independent entities and thus as a preparatory stage for the development of the concept of an impersonal quintessence (or *brahman*) of the manifest world.

The concept of *brahman* (neutr.) was of first-rate importance in the religious and philosophical speculations of the post-vedic period, and, as S. Dasgupta (1963^5, I, 20) remarked, it 'has been the highest glory for the Vedānta philosophy of later days'. In one sense it is antipodal to the idea of *īśvara*, yet in another sense it can be said to complement it, or perhaps even partially define it. For in the formulation of the notion of a personal god the idea of the omnipresent and omnitemporal ground of being is never quite lost sight of.

The idea of a personal deity is anticipated in the ṛgvedic conception of the 'unknown god' (M. Müller's phrase) eulogised in X.121, as also in the conception of Prajāpati, Dhātṛ, Viśvakarman, Tvaṣṭṛ and Puruṣa (see X.90). Whether or not one interprets these, according to some preconceived evolutionist system, as the culmination of a primitive polytheist medley, it is clear that by the time the bulk of the *Mahābhārata* had been composed the concept of *īśvara* was firmly lodged in the religious sector of Indian culture. The theism of the epic is largely analogous to that of the metric Upaniṣads, such as the *Śvetāśvatāra*- and the *Kaṭha-Upaniṣad* and not least the *Bhagavad-Gītā*. This highlights an interesting point, namely it brings out the close relation which exists between the concept of *īśvara*, *Sāṃkhya* ontological ideas and yogic practice. Their joint occurrence in the post-buddhist period is certainly remarkable and calls for an explanation.

B. Kumarappa (1934, 3), in a slightly different context, suggested that theological speculation was originally triggered off by the primary question 'Whence this universe?'. He thus linked up theism with cosmological and etiological considerations, which would seem to have the supportive evidence of the many creation theories in the *Upaniṣads*. But perhaps this is merely half the full answer. A different solution to this problem is possible if one places proper emphasis on the fact that it is not only the more speculative Sāṃkhya which is bound up with the *īśvara* concept, but also the age-old experimental tradition of Yoga. Basing myself on R. Otto's (1959) hypothesis of an innate capacity in man for numinous experiencing, I wish to propose that *īśvara* is essentially an *experimental construct* arrived at primarily on the basis of yogic self-absorption rather than pure theological ratiocination. In this respect it can be aligned with the other ontological categories of pre-classical Sāṃkhya and Yoga which, as I will show, are most appropriately understood as being phenomenological distillations of meditative-enstatic experiences. However, I hasten to emphasise that this line of argumentation in no way implies either an affirmation or a denial of the objective reference of any of these categories of experience.

It has not always been appreciated that theism is woven into the very fabric of *hindu* Yoga. Thus, in R. Garbe's (1894) opinion, Yoga is a theistic reinterpretation of the *nirīśvara* (atheistic) tradition of ancient Sāṃkhya. He speculated (p. 50) that this acceptance of *īśvara* into Yoga was the likely result of an effort to make Yoga more acceptable to the popular strata of society. H. Oldenberg (1915, 281) probed further: 'Did this belief originally pertain to Yoga as an essential element? Have Sāṃkhya and Yoga always been differentiated in the way the epic has it and as they are differentiated in their classical forms: as an atheistic and a theistic system respectively? This seems doubtful. The practice of Yoga obviously does not necessarily presuppose the notion of god [. . .]. Visible proof that a system greatly suffused with yogic elements could nonetheless reject the belief in god is supplied by the doctrine [. . .] of the Buddha.'

This stance has been challenged early on in the controversy by H. Jacobi (1923, 39), who wrote: 'This assertion of Īśvara has been interpreted as a concession of Yoga to Brahmanism, which is surely wrong; rather one should admire the audacity and the courage of a school of philosophy which, in the face of the prevalent atheism in philosophical and orthodox circles, dared to put forward the existence of Īśvara [. . .] as one of its doctrinal axioms.' H. Jacobi thus reaffirmed L. von Schroeder's (1887, 687) contention that 'Yoga has a distinct theistic character'.

This has been definitively confirmed by more recent research into the pre-classical configurations of the Sāṃkhya school of thought. In an outstanding contribution, K. B. R. Rao (1966) has conclusively demonstrated the intrinsic theistic nature of the pre-classical Sāṃkhya schools. His comprehensive study fully corroborates and consolidates F. Edgerton's (1924, 8) findings: 'Where, then, do we find that "original" atheistic view expressed? I believe: *nowhere*. A study of the epic and other early materials [. . .] has convinced me that there is not a single passage in which disbelief in Brahman or God is attributed to Sāṃkhya.'

H. Jacobi (1923) saw a connection between the employment of austerities (*tapas*) and the belief in *īśvara*. He pointed out that not infrequently the declared purpose of the fearful ascetic practices was to get the attention of a particular deity who, impressed and gratified with the *tapasvin*'s self-inflicted hardship and unflinching endurance, would bestow a boon on him. He mentioned in passing that in such a context the deity was generally known as *varada* or 'bestower of the boon'. He speculated (p. 29): 'For the popular conception at least, the grace of the deity was a necessary precondition for the recompense of ascetic exertion. It seems but natural that Yoga should adopt the recognition of Īśvara into its system.'

This view is reiterated in many modern studies, especially on the history of religions. Thus N. Smart (1968, 30), a representative proponent of this misconception, wrote: '. . . Yoga has borrowed a concept from popular religion and put it to a special use.' As he asserted elsewhere (1971, 163), Yoga is essentially an atheistic system. No reasons were supplied. At least H. Jacobi (1923) offered some kind of explanation even though it is unacceptable. For what his interpretation amounts to is the reduction of the conception of a personal god to one of two actors in a process of bargaining: the ascetic excels himself and is rewarded or 'paid off' by the deity. I do not contest that this may be exactly the essence of many of the ascetic 'deals' recorded in the epic. But I find it unsound reasoning to take this as a historical prelude to the act of grace (*prasāda*) spoken of in later Yoga. I prefer to understand such legends as folkloristic interpretations of a phenomenon which could well be a parameter of mystical experiencing: the ultimate crossing of the threshold of phenomenal existence interpreted as a transcendental act which appears to be initiated as it were from 'outside' or 'above'.

The idea implicit in H. Jacobi's (1923) suggestion that Patañjali in a way made a compromise to placate the orthodoxy is preposterous. Imputing to the famous Yoga teacher such hypocrisy, it is hardly surprising that his precise philosophical position has never been appraised adequately.

Less objectionable but similarly unconvincing is M. Müller's (1916[2], 326) psychological explanation. Rejecting the historical argument according to which Patañjali merely sought to appease the orthodox *brāhmaṇas*, M. Müller instead suggested that it was the natural human craving for a first cause which led Patañjali to the postulation of *īśvara*. If this were correct one would expect *īśvara* to have at least one definite cosmological function; yet 'the lord' is neither the creator nor sustainer or destroyer of the universe. The 'first cause' of which M. Müller spoke is, in Patañjali's system, the world ground or *prakṛti*, the eternally creative matrix of the manifest world.

Against the above historical and psychological explanations of the concept of *īśvara*, I wish to propose that its origins lie in the realm of yogic experiencing itself. This is also M. Eliade's (1973[3], 75) conclusion: 'Patañjali nevertheless had to introduce Īśvara into Yoga, for Īśvara was, so to speak, an experiential datum . . .'. This of course does not imply that Patañjali's formulation of the concept is a creation *ex nihilo*. It is obvious from a perusal of the *Mahābhārata*, especially certain portions of the twelfth *parvan*, that the conceptualisation of *īśvara* in Classical Yoga has its epic antecedents.

Philosophically the most important treatment of the theistic component in epic Yoga is to be found in section XII.296[1] of the critical edition of the *Mahābhārata*. Here *hiraṇyagarbha-yoga*[2] is dealt with, which K. B. R. Rao (1966, 278) wrongly identified as the philosophy of the epic Yoga system *par excellence*. However, this slip does not detract from the general merit of his acute analysis of this particular branch of Yoga. On the basis of P. M. Modi's (1932) earlier work, he succeeded in achieving a complete reinterpretation of the above passage, which has been lamentably misconstrued by F. Edgerton (1965) and others. He managed to reconstruct a good deal of the philosophy sketched in these extremely difficult and obscure verses.

Accepting, in principle, the general epic theories about the twenty-three evolutes of the unitary world-ground, the *hiraṇyagarbha* school of Yoga introduced the noteworthy distinction between the Self which has recovered its innate enlightenment, *viz*. the so-called *buddhyamāna*, and the ever-enlightened *buddha* or *prabuddha*. In comparison with the latter, *i.e.* god, the enlightened Self is said to be *abuddhimān* (see vs. 17). Thus there is no simple identification of the twenty-fifth *tattva*, *viz*. *buddhyamāna*, with the twenty-sixth, which is the supreme godhead. The latter principle is also referred to as *īśvara*, *mahā-ātman* and *avyakta-brahman*. The *buddhyamāna* is also called *puruṣa* and *buddha* (which confusingly enough is also applied to the twenty-sixth *tattva*). The twenty-fourth principle, which is the insentient world-ground, is known by the name of *prakṛti*, *abuddha*, *avyakta* and *apratibuddha*.

It is said of the *buddhyamāna* (see vs. 2) that it creates, upholds and withdraws the primary-constituents (*guṇa*) of the world-ground and that it 'knows' or apperceives the world-ground (see vs. 3) whilst itself being *nirguṇa* (see vs. 4) and hence 'unknown' by the *avyakta*. On the other hand, the *buddhyamāna* does not apperceive the lord (see vs. 6), who is pure, incomprehensible, eternal and always apperceiving (see vs. 7). This *mahā-ātman* or great being permeates both the visible and the invisible (see vs. 8). When the *buddhyamāna* or Self identifies itself with something that is external to its being, it is known as *avyakta-locana* (see vs. 10). Taking his cue from XII.296.18 (= XII.284.18 crit. ed.), K. B. R. Rao (1966, 282) interpreted this term as 'wearing the spectacles of *prakṛti*' or 'seeing through the *avyakta*' by means of the organ of cognition (which is *buddhi*) rather than understanding this interesting compound in the plain sense of 'seeing the *avyakta*'.

The goal of this Yoga is naturally also quite different from that enunciated in the contemporaneous Sāṃkhya and Pāñcarātra schools, which advocate a merger of the phenomenal self with the transcendental Self. This difference is evident from such phrases as *buddhatva* (XXI.296.11), *kevala-dharma* (vs. 12) or *kevalena samāgamya* (vs. 13). These appear to imply that the *buddhyamāna* attains to the 'estate' of the twenty-sixth principle without becoming identical with it. In other words, *īśvara* always remains transcendent (*para*). He never becomes involved with any of the lower *tattvas*. Thus emancipation can be said to be a condition of the *buddhyamāna qua* the *buddhyamāna* in the 'company' (*samiti*) of the lord (see XII.296.27 ff.).

The metaphysics of this prominent school of Yoga in epic times seemingly provided the paradigm for the peculiar ontology of Classical Yoga. This was first pointed out by P. M. Modi (1932, 81): 'The idea of God in the Yoga System was not arrived at by superimposing it on an atheistic Sāṃkhya System with twenty-five principles, but by distinguishing the Jīva from God on practical grounds.' This is endorsed by K. B. R. Rao (1966, 290): 'Probably the Epic Yoga lays the inchoate foundation for the classical Yoga conception of a detached Īśvara.' However, he felt compelled to remark (p. 291) that the conception of *īśvara* in the ancient *hiraṇyagarbha-yoga* is 'utterly naive and simple', since it depicts god as 'a motionless and frigid witness' who is not even interested in the *yogin*'s struggle for emancipation. He also deemed the more activist conception of god as expressed in the *Yoga-Bhāṣya* (I.25) a positive advance on this view. Evidently K. B. R. Rao's criticism is somewhat biased.

Although no mention is made in the relevant epic passage of the lord's soteriological function, one must nevertheless ask oneself why a need should have been felt to philosophically recognise the superlative status of *īśvara* if this concept would not somehow have had a compelling experiential basis. This line of argumentation would seem to be supported by the strictly pragmatic approach of Yoga, with its emphasis on experiment and personal verification. Nor is the absence of any reference in the above passage to the idea of grace or *prasāda*, which looms large in other contexts, a positive proof of its irrelevance in the yogic process as envisaged in *hiraṇyagarbha-yoga*.

A different hypothesis about the historical precursor of Classical Yoga was put forward by E. H. Johnston (1937). He proposed that 'the Sāṃkhya side of Patañjali's doctrine is based on the teaching of Pañcaśikha' (p. 9). His principal reason for this assertion was that Vyāsa, in his *Yoga-Bhāṣya*, cites Pañcaśikha on many occasions. Actually, Vyāsa himself nowhere mentions Pañcaśikha by name, but the appropriate identifications are exclusively supplied by Vācaspati Miśra, who is many generations later still. As P. Chakravarti (1951, 115) has made plausible, the quotations in question are probably from a work by Vārṣagaṇya. Also, in one instance at least, the *Yukti-Dīpikā*, which is older than the *Tattva-Vaiśāradī*, definitely contradicts Vācaspati Miśra, *viz.* in ascribing the fragment quoted in *Yoga-Bhāṣya* III.13 to Vārṣagaṇya and not to Pañcaśikha. Vārṣagaṇya, of course, is not an exponent of Yoga at all, but a renowned Sāṃkhya teacher (see *Mahābhārata* XII.306.57).

Patañjali's association with the *hiraṇyagarbha* school of Yoga is tentatively corroborated by the tradition preserved in the *Ahirbudhyna-Saṃhitā* (XII.3-38). The exact date of this intriguing work is still unsettled. E. H. Johnston (1937, 76, fn. 1) maintained that 'the system set out can be very little older than the *SK* [*Sāṃkhya-Kārikā*]'. F. O. Schrader (1916, 97) fixed its *terminus ad quem* at A.D. 800. On the other hand, since the *Ahirbudhnya-Saṃhitā* is aware of the three schools of Mahāyāna Buddhism – *viz. skandha-vāda* (= *sarvāsti-vāda*), *vijñāna-vāda* and *śūnya-vāda* – it cannot, in his opinion, be earlier than A.D. 300. As it mentions the *Jayākhyā-* and the *Sāttvata-Saṃhitā*, it must be later than these two important works. E. Krishnamacharya (1931) assigned the *Jayākhyā-Saṃhitā* on linguistic and palaeographic grounds to the middle of the fifth century. Hence we arrive at a date for the *Ahirbudhnya-Saṃhitā* between A.D. 500 and A.D. 800. In other words, it is definitely later than the *Yoga-Sūtra* and the *Sāṃkhya-Kārikā*. Consequently, we must treat its information about the lost Sāṃkhya treatise entitled *ṣaṣṭi-tantra* and about the Yoga of Hiraṇyagarbha with the necessary caution. Yet the relatively late date of the *Ahirbudhnya-Saṃhitā* need not mean that its knowledge of these ancient Yoga and Sāṃkhya tracts is necessarily unauthentic.

After this brief excursion into the epic antecedents of Classical Yoga, I will next scrutinise Patañjali's theological formulations. He defines 'the lord' (*īśvara*) in this way: *kleśa-karma-vipāka-āśayair-aparāmṛṣṭaḥ puruṣa-viśeṣa īśvaraḥ*, or 'The lord is a special Self untouched by the causes-of-affliction, [by] action [and its] fruit [and by] the deposit [of subliminal-activators]' (I.24). In the Yoga and Sāṃkhya ontology the entire spectrum of existence is analysed into the two primary modalities of Self (*puruṣa*) and non-self (*prakṛti*). The former embodies the principle of pure awareness roughly corresponding to the Kantian 'trans-intelligible subject', whereas the latter is the womb of all creation. P. Bowes (1971, 168) circumscribed these as the 'principle of consciousness' and the 'principle of materiality' respectively. Understandably *īśvara* could not but be included in the former category, as has been pointed out long ago by Vātsyāyana in his commentary to *Nyāya-Sūtra* IV.1.21.

Thus god is defined as a Self *sui generis*, and his separateness from the 'ordinary' transcendental Self or *puruṣa* is explained in negative terms: the lord is unaffected by any of the modifications which the ordinary *puruṣa* is subjected to by reason of his involvement with the world-ground and its products. To put it differently, *īśvara* at no time forsook, or will forsake, his perfect condition of transcendence as pure Being-Awareness. Because of his 'inactivity', by which is not meant mere abstention from action but perhaps the kind of condition which the *Bhagavad-Gītā* calls 'actionlessness' or *naiṣkarmya*, no *vipāka* (karmic fruition) ever accrues to him, and for the same reason he is also never subjected to the causes-of-affliction which are the natural concomitants of any implication in phenomenal existence.

This raises the question of whether Patañjali subscribed to the epic Yoga model of twenty-six principles. According to P. Chakravarti (1951, 66), Patañjali – even though envisaging a certain distinction between the ordinary Self and the Lord – does not make a radical enough distinction to be able to speak of the Lord as a wholly separate principle. Possibly this whole issue is misconceived. Unlike the epic teachers, Patañjali does not turn the number of fundamental ontological categories (*tattva*) into a *principium individuationis* by which he can conveniently contrast his own school with other traditions. He does not even employ the term *tattva* in that specific sense. On the contrary, his ontological model can be regarded as a decisive break with this numerative trend of the epic schools. Nor do Vyāsa and Vācaspati Miśra give this issue any attention, but simply accept Patañjali's novel cosmo-genetic schema without relating it to the prolonged controversy about twenty-five *versus* twenty-six principles.

Patañjali was possibly wiser than his predecessors, the epic *īśvara-vādins*, who, misunderstanding the Sāṃkhya teaching about the *buddhyamāna*, unjustifiedly dubbed their adversaries *an-īśvara-vādins* and perhaps unduly inflated the significance of their own doctrine of a twenty-sixth principle, *i.e.* the totally undynamic *īśvara*.

M. Müller (1916⁴, 321) remarked that the lord 'may be *primus inter pares*, but as one of the Purushas, he is but one among his peers. He is a little more than a god, but he is certainly not what we mean by God.' Yet Patañjali's definition of *īśvara* implies that he is not only a special and unique species of Self but that he also has a positive aspect. This is clear from I.25–I.28: *tatra niratiśayaṃ sarva-jña-bījam*; *pūrveṣām-api guruḥ kālena anavacchedāt*; *tasya vācakaḥ praṇavaḥ*; *taj-japas-tad-artha-bhāvanam*. This can be rendered as follows: 'In this [*īśvara*] the seed of omniscience is unsurpassed. He was also the teacher of the former [*yogins*], since there is no temporal limitation [for him]. His signature is the *praṇava* [*i.e. oṃ*]. The recitation of that [*praṇava*] [leads to] the realisation of its meaning.' These statements must be read in conjunction with the concept of *īśvara-praṇidhāna* or 'devotion to the Lord'.

Aphorism I.25 is of special interest, as it has always been understood as a 'proof' of the existence of god. Thus the *Yoga-Bhāṣya* (I.25) has:

yatra kāṣṭhā-prāptir-jñānasya sa sarva-jñaḥ sa ca puruṣa-viśeṣa iti, or 'In whom the limit of knowledge is reached, he is all-knowing and he is a special Self'. By 'seed' Vācaspati Miśra understands 'cause' (*kāraṇa*), whereas Vijñāna Bhikṣu, in his *Yoga-Vārttika*, explains it as 'mark' (*liṅga*). Our 'supra-sensuous grasping' (*ati-indriya-grahaṇa*), as Vācaspati Miśra observes, depends on the degree to which *tamas* obscures *sattva*.[3] The moderate capacity for knowledge displayed by the worldling contains the seed of higher knowledge and, even, omniscience. There comes an upper limit which cannot be surpassed, and this is the omniscience of the lord.

As G. M. Koelman (1970, 61) correctly noted: 'The absolute extension of the lord's knowledge is unambiguously asserted. But there is no word, no insinuation even that the lord's knowledge is different in essence, is a more perfect way of knowing.' Vyāsa explains the unexcellable knowledge of *īśvara* as the result of the utter purity of the *sattva* reflecting his transcendental Awareness. His knowledge extends to all objects and all periods, and it is this which distinguishes him from such seers as Kapila or the Buddha.

It is difficult to decide whether or not these observations by the classical exegetes were in fact intended as a kind of 'proof' of the existence of god. Patañjali himself, again, is far too concise to win such an interpretation from *sūtra* I.25. Probably it simply refers to the fact that, in contrast with the awareness of the ordinary *puruṣa*, the *īśvara*'s awareness is perfectly continuous, that is to say, uninterrupted by *prakṛti*, since *īśvara* at no time and not even for an instant falls victim to nescience (*avidyā*). Maybe aphorism I.25 entails not so much a grading of omniscience, which would make little sense, as a statement about the fact that what constitutes a potential for the ordinary being is a permanent actuality for *īśvara*. I cannot agree with S. Radhakrishnan's (1951[6], II, 369) assertion that 'Patañjali proves the omniscience of God by means of the law of continuity, which must have an upper limit'. Instead I prefer to see in Patañjali's cryptic statement a parallel to the Mahāyāna notion of the *tathāgata-garbha* as the seed of consummate enlightenment, temporarily obscured by defilements of a cognitive and conative nature, *viz.* *vikalpa* (conceptual construction) and *abhiniveśa* (mundane attachment), whilst in reality it is transcendental and *nirvikalpa* (trans-conceptual). As long as this seed has not sprouted, cognition is distorted and things are not seen as they are (*yathā-bhūta*).[4]

That the lord is not conceptualised as a being who is of complete irrelevance to mankind clearly emerges from I.26, where *īśvara* is called 'the teacher of the former [*yogins*]'. This is in keeping with the traditional pre-classical interpretation of the concept of god as expressed, for instance, in the following stanza from the *Bhagavad-Gītā* (IV.1): *imaṃ vivasvate yogaṃ proktavān-aham-avyayam, vivasvān-manave prāha manur-īkṣvākave'bravīt*, or 'To Vivasvat I expounded this imperishable Yoga; Vivasvat related it to Manu; Manu told it to Īkṣvāku.' Unless one presumes this doctrine to be no more than a forced concession to revealed tradition (*śruti*), which would be incongruous with Patañjali's generally self-reliant approach, there is one difficult question which calls for an answer.

This is: how can a perfectly transcendental being assume a teaching role? Vyāsa, in his *Yoga-Bhāṣya* (I.25), attempts to solve this problem by introducing anthropomorphic features: *tasya-ātma-anugraha-abhāve'pi bhūta-anugrahaḥ prayojanaṃ, jñāna-dharma-upadeśena kalpa-pralaya-mahā-pralayeṣu saṃsāriṇaḥ puruṣa-anuddhariṣyāmi-iti, tathā ca-uktam-ādi-vidvān-nirmāṇa-cittam-adhiṣṭhāya kāruṇyād-bhagavān parama-ṛṣir-āsuraye jijñāsamānāya-tantraṃ provāca-iti*, or 'Although he has no [feeling of] self-gratification, [the lord's] motive is the gratification of beings: "By instruction in knowledge and virtue, at the dissolution [of the world] [at the end of] a world-age [or] at the great dissolution [or the entire universe], I will uplift the Selves [immersed] in conditioned-existence." And likewise it has been said: "The first knower, assuming a created mind out of compassion, the exalted, supreme seer declared this teaching to Āsuri who desired to know." '

This passage epitomises the popular and orthodox belief that *īśvara* is the author of the Vedas by whose teachings the staunch believer transcends all ill. Within the framework of Patañjali's philosophy such an interpretation makes little sense. A more sophisticated solution is called for which does not in any way interfere with the definition of *īśvara* as transcendence *per se*. The classical exegetes are of no help here. Their interpretations of the nature of *īśvara* are exclusive attempts to somehow relate his existence to the mechanisms of the world-ground and to the destinies of the sentient beings ensnared by *prakṛti*.

If one excludes the possibility of *īśvara* actively entering into a teaching situation by mysteriously phenomenalising himself, there remains only one logical alternative, and this is that his role as a teacher is in fact entirely passive. His very existence is a sufficient challenge to the *yogin* who either has come through faith (*śraddhā*) to believe in him, or whose spiritual discipline has brought him to the margins of conditioned existence where experiential proof of his existence may be found. In other words, *īśvara* is the archetypal *yogin* who 'instructs' by his sheer being.[5] Pressing this metaphor still further, one could say that 'communication' between him and the aspiring *yogin* is possible by reason of the ontic co-essentiality of god and the inmost nucleus of man, *viz.* the Self (*puruṣa*). M. Eliade (1973[3], 74) pertinently circumscribed this with the phrase 'metaphysical sympathy'.

On the transcendental level the relation between *īśvara* and *puruṣa* is one of 'enclosure' by coalescence; the Self is eclipsed by the being of *īśvara*. Empirically, however, the relation is a one-way affair in which the believing *yogin* emulates *īśvara*'s condition, which is co-essential with the condition of his inmost Self. This is the idea implicit in the concept of *īśvara-praṇidhāna*, which is a channelling of one's emotive and cognitive life to god by endeavouring to 'simulate' his unconditioned nature. For the purpose of this *imitatio Dei* the *yogin* symbolises god in the form of the *praṇava* which is the sacred phoneme *oṃ*. As Vyāsa, in his *Yoga-Bhāṣya* (I.27), aptly points out, this symbolisation is not due to convention (*saṅketa*), but the connection between *īśvara* and *oṃ* is a natural (inherent) and permanent one. In other words, *oṃ* is an experience rather than an arbitrary verbal label. It is a true symbol charged with numinous power. Experienceable in deep meditation, it is a sign of the omnipresence of *īśvara* as manifest on the level of sound. Access to this experience is gained, paradoxically, through the vocal or silent recitation of *oṃ*. Thus *oṃ* is both expedient and goal. In other words, the human voice is employed to reproduce a 'sound' which is continually 'recited' by the universe itself – an idea which in the Pythagorean school came to be known as the 'harmony of the spheres'. On the Indian side it led to the development of the Yoga of sound (*nāda-yoga*).[6]

By now it should have become evident that, notwithstanding the precarious philosophical interpretation of *īśvara* in Classical Yoga, god is of no mean importance in its practical sphere. I cannot therefore endorse G. M. Koelman's (1970, 57) contention that it 'is striking how the mention of the *īśvara* in the Yoga Sutras is quite casual' and that we 'could very well cut out the sutras relating to the Lord, without in any way impairing the systematic coherence of the *Pātañjala Yoga*, without even leaving a trace of the excision' (p. 58). This is of course a recapitulation of R. Garbe's (1917[2], 149) view, which, *inter alia*, was also accepted by S. Radhakrishnan (1951[6], II, 371, fn. 3) and N. Smart (1968, 30).[7]

G. M. Koelman (1970, 63 f.) elucidated his position further: 'If we said that the *īśvara* does not answer any logical need in the *Pātañjala Yoga*, we do not maintain that either Patañjali himself or the Yogis in general cannot be true devotees of the *īśvara*. The only thing we mean to say is that the whole Yoga philosophy and the psychological technique of liberation it stands for are atheistic in nature. If some one yogi, even if all yogis, did admit *īśvara*, as somehow God, this would be due not to Yoga doctrine, but to the yogis' individual religious dispositions. We might say that *Pātañjala Yoga* technique prescinds from whether someone admits a God or denies him.'

Yet, strangely enough, in the very next sentence the author stated: 'We believe that *Pātañjala Yoga* is essentially theistic. But as G. R. F. Oberhammer has proved [*sic!*], the *Pātañjala* doctrine of the Supreme Lord had to express itself in terms of a philosophical school, the *Sāṅkhya* School, which has no room for God.' Despite his unusual objectivity on other points, the author – a Jesuit – apparently found it difficult to suspend his preconception of what god ought or ought not to be.

The fact is that the doctrine of *īśvara* is an integral component of the philosophy of Classical Yoga and that, moreover, *īśvara* figures prominently in the practice structure of Yoga, and any attempt to exorcise this concept would amount to a crippling of both the theoretical superstructure and the practical substructure of Yoga. It is correct, as M. Eliade (1973[3], 73) observed, that *īśvara* is a god only for the *yogins*, the spiritually awakened who are prepared to take him as their *Vorbild*. Before him, P. Deussen (1920[3], 545) drew the following interesting parallel: 'There is here a similarity with the system of Epicurus; like his gods, īśvara in Yoga does not interfere in the least in mundane affairs or in the destinies of the soul. But just as Epicurus was unwilling to do without the gods as ideals of happiness, even though they dwell in total isolation from the world processes in the inter mundi, so also in Yoga devotion to God, *īśvara-praṇidhāna* [. . .] is recommended as one of the several means to promote Yoga meditation.'

However, since it is implied in the philosophy of Classical Yoga, as in all other *darśanas*, that the *summum bonum* of human life is to transcend contingent existence, god can, and in terms of this ethical model should, be meaningful also to the laity. Shocking as the attenuated theism of Classical Yoga must be to the committed deist, it is a curious fact that rather cognate views can be found in the writings of some of the greatest intellectual mystics, such as Meister Eckehart and Plotinus. This may be instructive in that it entails the warning not to look at this question from a purely theoretical point of view but to take cognisance also of the realities of spiritual practice and of experiential 'verification'.

II
The Self (*puruṣa*)

Like the notion of *īśvara* the concept of the Self (*puruṣa*) is not purely a hypothetico-deductive postulate. It is best understood as circumscribing a particular yogic experience of the numinous. This 'experience', however, is not of the nature of what is ordinarily meant by this term. Owing to the radical dualism between Self and non-self (or *prakṛti*), as envisaged in Classical Yoga, there can strictly speaking be no experience *of* the Self at all. This holds true of *īśvara* as well, being defined as he is as a *puruṣa sui generis*. As will be shown, Patañjali does make certain provisions, though, which allow one to speak of a 'vision of the Self' (*puruṣa-khyāti*) or 'Self gnosis' (*puruṣa-jñāna*).

In view of the experiential derivation of the concept of *puruṣa* proposed here, all explanations which seek to establish the *logical* necessity of the Self within the conceptual lattice of Classical Yoga, or which try to make a case for the *theoretical* inadequacy of this doctrine, must be relegated to a subsidiary position. The preeminently practical orientation of Yoga has not always been duly appreciated by Western scholars. Thus when R. Garbe (1917^2, 356) insisted that the *puruṣa* is primarily a philosophical postulate inferred from empirical data, he blatantly ignored the fact that, whatever role ratiocination may play in Classical Sāṃkhya, its foundations are, like those of Classical Yoga, to be found among the diverse traditions of *consciousness technology* current at the time of the *Mahābhārata*. The classical proofs adduced for the existence of the Self must therefore be looked upon as afterthoughts to consolidate what originally constituted an experiential (but not empirically observable) datum.

Nonetheless, the 'rationalisation' and 'moralisation' – R. Otto's (1959) terms – of the encounter with the numinous in Yoga are potent in themselves, because they are the building blocks of the soteriological formulations in the doctrinal structure of both Classical Yoga and the Sāṃkhya of Īśvara Kṛṣṇa. Treating the interrelation between Self and non-self, A. Bharati (1970^3, 204) offered another suggestion which lies midway between the experiential and the rationalistic answer. He regarded the *puruṣa* as a 'postulate of intuition rather than of discursive reasoning'. Elsewhere (p. 16) he explained his use of the term 'intuition', which he sets off from gnosis or *jñāna*, and consequently one must appraise this interpretation as inadequate as the rationalist conjecture.[1]

The history of the word *puruṣa* and its association with the experience of the numinous in Yoga is a long and interesting one. It is remarkable that the Yoga and Sāṃkhya traditions should have adopted this designation rather than the synonym *ātman*, which enjoys such a great popularity in the Vedānta schools of thought. The etymological derivation of the word has given rise to a considerable amount of speculation. Native Indian tradition proffers several, more or less fanciful, etymologies. The oldest reference is to be found in the *Atharvaveda* (X.2.28, 30) which has a pun on the word *pur* or 'citadel' to the effect of stating that *pur-uṣa* is a derivative of it. This etymology is also mentioned in the *Mahābhārata* (XII.294.37), following *Bṛhadāraṇyaka-Upaniṣad* (II.5.18), where *puruṣa* is analysed into 'he who lies (*śete*) in the "citadel" (*pura*)' of the unmanifest world-ground. In the *Nirukta* (VII.13) a further derivation from *pur* + $\sqrt{}$*sad* (= *puriṣāda*) and also from $\sqrt{}$*pṛ* ('to fill') is suggested. Another, less popular, etymology is given in the *Bṛhadāraṇyaka-Upaniṣad* (I.4.1), where the word is broken down into *purva* + $\sqrt{}$*uṣ* ('to burn'). According to R. Garbe (1917^2, 356) the correct etymology of the word *puruṣa* and its synonyms *puṃs* and *pumāṃs* is the one suggested by E. Leumann ([?], 10–12), namely the compound *pu-vṛṣa*, both components of which signify 'man'.[2]

In its earliest recorded conception, *puruṣa* stands both for the mortal 'person'[3] and, more significantly, for the cosmic creator who, like the giant Ymir in teutonic mythology, is the *causa materialis* and the *causa efficiens* of the manifest universe; he is the demiurge *and* the primordial substance from which the world is fashioned. This double role is possible because the act of creation is understood as the self-dismemberment of the macrocosmic Person. Symbolically this is interpreted as the primal sacrifice (*yajña*), of archetypal importance to the pan-Indian sacrificial cult. In most instances, this gigantic *puruṣa* is thought of as transcending the world which he emits from his own body.[4] It is this cosmogonic model which was destined to exert a decisive influence on subsequent thought in India, as can readily be appreciated from a study of the *Bhagavad-Gītā* and other works of the Pāñcarātra school, as well as the memorable passage in *Bṛhadāraṇyaka-Upaniṣad* (I.2),[5] where the primordial Being, tired of its loneliness, decides to create an *alter ego* out of itself.[6]

In the *Chāndogya-Upaniṣad* (VIII.10.1) a record of popular psychological theory has been preserved according to which the *puruṣa*, conceived as a 'mannikin', departs from the body of the sleeping person. This notion of an indwelling 'ghost' is part of many folk philosophies, and it figures, among other ancient non-Indian literary documents, in Homer's *Odyssey* (*e.g.* X.493). E. H. Johnston (1937, 41 ff.) speculated that the later 'soul theory', as he called the doctrine of *puruṣa*, was arrived at through the gradual fusion of the primitive notion of an immaterial principle or principles animating the human body and of the equally archaic notion of a separate psyche which acts as the carrier of a person's *post mortem* identity. He thought (p. 43) that the *Ṛgveda* 'contains traces of both conceptions and of the beginning of their amalgamation'. This historical approach, which treats conceptualisations of a different type and degree of complexity as causally linkable and chemically mixable substances, as it were, is entirely inapt and inconclusive. One can take this as a typical instance of what A. N. Whitehead (1938[8], 66) called the 'fallacy of misplaced concreteness'.

Following up the development of the concept of *puruṣa*, E. H. Johnston (1937) found that in the early metric *Upaniṣads* and in the *Bhagavad-Gītā* (except for chapters XIII–XVIII) *puruṣa* denotes the individual psyche. He conjectured (p. 53) that this term replaced the concept of *ātman kṣetrajña* in the older texts. He also maintained that those epic passages which equate the *puruṣa* with *ātman* belong to a more recent period.

J. W. Hauer (1958, 64) made the interesting point that the frequency of the word *puruṣa* is higher in the *Atharvaveda* than in the *Ṛgveda*, which far more often employs the term *ātman*. He even went so far as to suggest that the word *puruṣa* is specific to the *vrātya* tradition as recorded in the *Atharvaveda* (see especially book XV) and that it came to be introduced into the doctrinal sphere of orthodox Brāhmaṇism as a result of the large-scale conversions of these *vrātyas*.

The heterodox origin of *puruṣa* is in fact strongly indicated by the fact that the ancient litany on Rudra, the god of the *vrātyas*, *viz.* the so-called *Śatarudriya* found in the *Kāṭhaka-Saṃhitā* (XVII.11–17; cf. XXI.6) represents, according to J. W. Hauer, the oldest version of the famous *gāyatrī-mantra*. It links up Rudra with *puruṣa*: *tad-puruṣāya vidmahe mahā-devāya dhīmahi tan-no rudraḥ pracodayāt*, or: 'This [litany] we have invented for the Puruṣa; let us meditate the great god; may Rudra promote us this [meditation]'.[7]

H. Oldenberg (1915, 224) made this pertinent observation: 'It is significant that linguistic usage tends to connect *ātman* with the genitive case in order to express whose Ātman is referred to, whereas *purusha* occurs more often in conjunction with a locative in order to indicate wherein this Purusha dwells. In view of this I would suspect that the preference for the designation Purusha for the spiritual principle in Sāṃkhya is related to the strict separation and confrontation, peculiar to this system, between the spirit and nature.' I am not sure to what extent this proposition is valid, but certainly *puruṣa* tends to be associated, if not with spatial metaphors, then with the related idea of rulership and proprietorship. This is quite evident in the phraseology of the *Yoga-Sūtra*, which on this point reflects the general trend of the upaniṣadic period.

Patañjali employs the term *puruṣa* altogether eight times (*viz.* I.16, 24; III.35 twice; III.49, 55; IV.18, 34). He also avails himself of a number of synonyms such as *draṣṭṛ* (I.3; II.17, 20; IV.23), *svāmin* (II.23), *grahītṛ* (I.41), *dṛg-śakti* (II.6), *dṛśi* (II.25), *dṛśi-mātra* (II.20), *prabhu* (IV.18), *citi* (IV.22), *citi-śakti* (IV.34) and *para* (IV.24). With the exception of the word *para* ('the other') these are all 'loaded' terms in so far as they are modelled on the empirical relations of perceiving, cognising and owning and for the sake of communication ascribe a content to something which is by definition without all differentiae (*nir-guṇa*) and hence strictly speaking incommunicable in words. The full latitude of the meaning of *puruṣa* is brought out when one maps the above synonyms in the manner of the diagram.

metaphor of otherness

para

metaphor of seeing	*draṣṭṛ* *dṛg-śakti* *dṛśi* *dṛśi-mātra*	PURUṢA	*svāmin* *prabhu* *grahītṛ*	metaphor of owning

citi
citi-śakti

metaphor of cognising

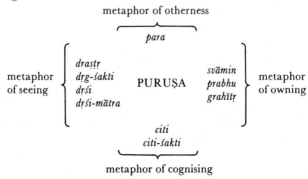

If one were to place the concept of *īśvara* into this semantic grid, it would have to be accommodated to the far right by virtue of the strong connotation of 'lordship' attached to this term. Most of these synonyms of the word *puruṣa* belong to the old stock of yogic terminology and occur already in the metric Upaniṣads and the *Mahābhārata*, but *dṛśi*, *dṛśi-mātra*, *dṛg-śakti*, *citi* and *citi-śakti* are more recent coinages which may possibly have originated under the influence of Mahāyāna Buddhism.

Nowhere in the *Yoga-Sūtra* is there a full-fledged definition of the concept of *puruṣa*, and the most probable reason for this is that by the time of the composition of Patañjali's *vade mecum* its precise meaning was perfectly evident. The opposite must have been true of the concept of *īśvara* which Patañjali carefully demarcates from its popular usage in the sense of 'creator'. From the few references in the *Yoga-Sūtra* it is clear beyond doubt that the concept of *puruṣa* is remarkably akin to certain conceptions delineated in the epic and other pre-classical Sanskrit works.[8] It expresses the notion of man's 'transcendental identity', here rendered with 'Self' or 'transintelligible subject', as distinct from the world-ground (*prakṛti*) both in its noumenal form as *pradhāna* and in its manifest form as the objective universe (*dṛśya*). The Self is an aspatial and atemporal reality which stands in no conceivable relation to the composite world of phenomena nor to their transcendental source. It is sheer awareness as opposed to consciousness-of and in this respect is the exact antithesis to the world-ground which is by definition insentient. This Self is considered the authentic being of man.

Since the mental apparatus, with its consciousness-of, is regarded as an evolute of the world-ground, the Self is necessarily also quite distinct from the mind (*citta*). Viewed psychologically, the Self is the 'seer' (*draṣṭṛ*) of the on-going psychomental processes or *vṛtti* (see I.3). As long as the empirical consciousness is operative and man's transcendental identity is obscured, this watchman is said to be 'of the same form' (*sārūpya*) as the psychomental whirls. This is to say, the loss of authenticity is due to the shifting identifications within the discontinuous states of experience: 'I am this sensation; I am that thought', etc. This perpetual process of constructing false identities is known as *asmitā* or 'I-am-ness'. It is this power, generated by 'nescience' (*avidyā*), which is responsible for the erection of man's inner world, *i.e.* his motivations, cognitive schemata and emotive response patterns and so forth.

The Self is set apart from all these mechanisms which are founded on the energetic character of the primary constituents of the world-ground, the so-called *guṇas*. Properly speaking, the *puruṣa* is neither an actor nor a passive enjoyer of the experiences which occur in the mind, even though some Sāṃkhya works speak of it metaphorically as the 'enjoyer' (*bhoktṛ*) of all experiences.[9] The Self does not intend, feel or think. The involvement with the discontinuous contents of consciousness, as implied by the phrase *sārūpya*, is merely an apparent one. It is 'affected' (*parāmṛṣṭa*) by the *kleśa-karma-vipāka-āśaya* sequence only in so far as these factors are instrumental in cluttering the empirical consciousness and thus in relinquishing its capacity for emptying itself, which is the only way in which the presentation of the transcendental Self to the mind can take place.

The 'correlation' (*saṃyoga*) between the 'seer' and the 'seen' (see II.17) is a peculiar one and ranks among the most problematic issues of the dualistic metaphysics of Yoga and Sāṃkhya; for it is difficult to comprehend how the Self, which is defined as 'mere seeing' (*dṛśi-mātra*) and 'pure' (*śuddha*), can apperceive the presented-ideas (*pratyaya*) as stated in aphorism II.20. We are told that the mental on-goings (*vṛtti*) are always apperceived *because* the *puruṣa* does not suffer any alteration but it is a perfect continuum (see IV.18).

M. Bowes (1971, 169) summed up the situation in this way: 'Indian philosophers, when faced with the objection that there is no such thing as consciousness as such, meaning that there is no empirical experience of such a thing, stress that even if all consciousness is consciousness of something there must be a function called "consciousness" to be conscious of this something. Many would object no doubt that this is hypostatising consciousness which arises only in a particular context of contact with objects and which is not to be thought of as an entity by itself, but the Indians claim that consciousness performs a distinct function, that of manifestation (equivalent to Sartre's revelation and Husserl's constitution function) of the object it is conscious of as well as of itself – a function which cannot be performed by anything which is non-conscious and so it must be thought of as there, as a reality of a distinct sort.'

For Patañjali this puzzle is no puzzle at all, but an eminently practical issue. As long as the 'correlation' (*saṃyoga*) between Self and world obtains, there is also suffering (*duḥkha*). Since the root of this correlation, or rather phantom correlation, between Self and non-self is nescience (*avidyā*), it is this which must be terminated. The prescribed expedient for the removal of the correlation condition is *viveka-khyāti*, the 'vision of discernment', a high-level enstasy which eliminates all one's false identities not by way of mere intellectual acrobatics but in a process of clarification and purification of consciousness. First the mind is withdrawn from the external stimuli, then all presented-ideas are obliterated and ultimately the subliminal traces (*vāsanā*) themselves are rooted out, which amounts to the total dispersion of the consciousness-of (*citta*).

Ordinary experience is possible only on account of the massive identity confusion arising from the overpowering influence of the subliminal traces which habitually throw the consciousness outside itself, thus forcing it to gather in continually new impressions, thereby replenishing the stock of subliminal traces (*vāsanā*) in the depths of the mind. In other words, the fundamental confusion about man's true identity is built into the psychomental organism whose growth and decay the individualised consciousness is witnessing. In fact, without this cognitive mix-up no experience would be possible.

Experiencing, called *bhoga* in aphorism III.35, is an intrapsychic process which does not actively involve the Self; the *puruṣa* simply apperceives the presented-ideas in the experiencing mind. Patañjali promulgates an extreme dualism when he insists that the Self and the most translucent aspect of the consciousness complex, the *sattva*, are eternally 'unmixed' (*asaṃkīrṇa*) (see III.35), and that precisely because of this perfect separateness the recovery of Self-authenticity is at all possible.[10]

Parenthetically it may be observed that by reason of the professed transphenomenal nature of the Self any qualitative ascription is, in the last analysis, tantamount to a falsification. This is as true of the description of *puruṣa* in terms of awareness (see *citi*, *citi-śakti*) as it is of the more obvious tropological predications. Unlike the anonymous author of the *Sāṃkhya-Sūtra*, Patañjali does not seem to favour negative descriptions of the nature of the Self but prefers, as we have seen above, metaphors of seeing, cognising and owning which are in keeping with his psychological rather than metaphysical approach.

One last important point remains to be discussed. This is the controversial question of the singularity or plurality of the Self as conceived in Classical Yoga. M. Eliade (1973³, 32–3) gave vent to the popular view on this matter when claiming about Sāṃkhya and Yoga that they 'affirm that there are as many *puruṣas* as there are human beings. And each of these *puruṣas* is a monad, is completely isolated; for the Self can have no contact either with the world around it (derived from *prakṛti*) or with other spirits. The cosmos, then, is people with these eternal, free, unmoving *puruṣas* – monads between which no communication is possible.'

Apart from the objection which one may wish to raise against M. Eliade's use of concepts such as 'monad' and 'communication' and also against his metaphor of the Selves' populating the cosmos,[11] another more serious criticism must be brought against his unquestioning acceptance of the testimony of rival schools which ascribe to Yoga the doctrine of the plurality of the transcendental Selves. He obviously relied in his judgement on the work of his teacher, S. Dasgupta (1930, 167), and others. But is this doctrine really a part of Patañjali's system of thought?

There can be no question that this strange doctrine is part and parcel of the philosophy expounded in the commentarial literature on the *Yoga-Sūtra* and also in Īśvara Kṛṣṇa's *Sāṃkhya-Kārikā*. The latter text has a stanza (18) which reads as follows: *jana-maraṇa-karaṇānāṃ pratiniyamād-ayugapat-pravṛtteś-ca, puruṣa-bahutvaṃ siddhaṃ trai-guṇya-viparyayāc-ca-eva*, 'The multiplicity of the Self is established by reason of the idiosyncracy[12] of [a person's] birth, death [and] deed[13] and because of non-simultaneous activity and also on account of the alteration in the *guṇa*-triad'. That the word *bahutva* in this stanza does not merely signify 'duplicity' but 'multiplicity' is borne out by the phrase *prati-puruṣa-vimokṣa-artham* or 'for the sake of the release of every (*prati*) Self' in verse 46 of the same work. The word *prati*, a favourite expression with Īśvara Kṛṣṇa (see vss. 5, 31, 37) has consistently the sense of 'every, each' in his *Sāṃkhya-Kārikā*.

The word *bahutva* is derived from *bahu*, meaning 'abundant, much', and it signifies 'multiplicity, multitude'. In the *Mahābhārata* the cognate *nānātva* is generally employed to express the idea of 'manifoldness'. There is, however, at least one instance in which *bahudhā* is used (*viz*. XII.296.2).[14] According to K. B. R. Rao's (1966, 278) analysis of this verse, either the idea of the plurality of Selves is implied in this passage or the *duplicity* of the Self (as *budhyamāna* and *buddha*). Previously F. Edgerton (1924) held such a view to be entirely untenable. As C. A. F. Rhys Davids (1936³, 146) noted long ago: 'A heresy so startling would have needed to be rubbed in, as it is not.' F. Edgerton (1924) severely criticised E. W. Hopkins (1901) for grossly misinterpreting the epic passage XII.303.12:

avyakta-ekatvam-ity-āhur-nānātvaṃ puruṣas-tathā sarva-bhūta-dayā-vantaḥ kevalaṃ jñānam-āsthitāḥ.

E. W. Hopkins (1901, 123):

Those who have the religion of compassion . . . say that there is unity in the Unmanifest but a plurality of spirits.

F. Edgerton (1924, 26):

It is a unity in the Unmanifest; so they explain the plurality (of the manifest, empiric universe) – men who, having compassion for all beings, resort to pure knowledge.

K. B. R. Rao (1966, 237):

Men who are compassionate with all beings, and who have resorted to *kevala jñāna*, i.e. the knowledge of the Absolute, say that the Avyakta is *eka* and also *nāna*.

F. Edgerton made the point that the phrase 'plurality of spirits' would require either *puruṣa-nānātvam* or *nānātvaṃ puruṣānām*. In his conviction the epic view coincides with that of the metric Upaniṣads, which is one 'of a plurality in the empiric, finite world, but an underlying unity, realized by the enlightened, in which there is no longer any plurality, nor any consciousness, the attribute of plurality' (p. 25).

S. Dasgupta (1930, 167) argued on the basis of aphorism II.22 that Patañjali recognised a plurality of transcendental Selves. In this he followed the cues provided in the *Yoga-Bhāṣya* and especially in the *Tattva-Vaiśāradī*. But what does this aphorism really convey? The Sanskrit text runs as follows: *kṛta-arthaṃ prati-naṣṭam-api anaṣṭaṃ tad-anya-sādhāraṇatvāt* or 'Though [the objective world] has ceased for [the one whose] purpose is accomplished, it has not ceased [altogether], since it is common to [all] the other [empirical selves].'

It cannot be conclusively shown on the strength of this aphorism alone that Patañjali subscribed to the doctrine of plurality. Nor are there any other statements in his work which would vindicate such a view. I am therefore inclined to read this *sūtra* in the spirit of the pre-classical tradition where *kṛta-artha* also denotes the person who has become the Self, *i.e.* who has recovered Self-authenticity, beyond all plurality.[15]

Availing himself of the stock arguments of the Sāṃkhya thinkers, S. Dasgupta (1930, 167 f.) saw an epistemological problem here. He asked how, in view of the postulated reality of *prakṛti*, one single *puruṣa* of equal reality could possibly be responsible for all the cognitive processes occurring in the multiple real organisms. He drew attention to the viewpoint of Advaita-Vedānta according to which the Self is at least not identified with the real experiencing subject, but which asserts that the notions of experiencing, etc., are all false, *i.e.* produced by the illusive action of *māyā* (which is itself inscrutable or *anirvacanīya*). He contended that if indeed only one *puruṣa* were 'associated' with the many psychosomatic entities, the release of a single being would imply the simultaneous release of all others. However, these are lame arguments, since the process of emancipation is a prakṛtic event which effects only a particular spatio-temporal entity, whereas the Self is *ex hypothesi* neither ever in bondage nor in need of liberation.

Assuming that Patañjali did not maintain that there are innumerable Self monads which inhabit some acosmic dimension, it must next be asked how this interpretation affects the conception of *īśvara* in his system. For *īśvara* is defined as a 'special Self' untouched by the causes-of-affliction (*kleśa*), by the propelling force of *karman* and so on. It may be thought that aphorism I.24 tabernacles the idea that the ordinary *puruṣa* is somehow 'touched' by the *kleśas*, etc., which would be an indirect confirmation of the doctrine of plurality. But there can be no question of the transcendental Self – be it *īśvara* or not – ever being affected in the literal sense by the causes-of-affliction or any other prakṛtic phenomenon. The phrase *kleśa-karma-vipāka-āśayair-aparāmṛṣṭaḥ* must therefore be applicable as much to the ordinary *puruṣa* as to *īśvara*. Unless one wants to stretch this aphorism beyond its capacity, it does not appear to entail either any real inconsistency, or a hidden reference to the notion that there are multiple Selves and that *īśvara* is *primus inter pares* as M. Müller (1916[4], 325) argued.

Thus Patañjali seems to have promulgated a variant of the pre-classical epic Yoga tradition which affirms the basic singularity of the transcendental Self. Furthermore, he apparently also accepted the theistic conception of his predecessors who understood *īśvara* as eclipsing the *puruṣa*. Where he differs from them is in his insistence on the absolute separateness of *puruṣa* and *prakṛti* – thus developing the dualistic trends in the *Mahābhārata* and the metric Upaniṣads into a full-fledged dualism with the transintelligible subject on the one side and the objective universe on the other. Philosophically unattractive, this Cartesian dichotomy is of considerable practical relevance.

III
The Structure of the World (*prakṛti*)

The third of the transcendental principles which together constitute the tripod of the conceptual edifice of Classical Yoga is *prakṛti*. The word is composed of the preposition *pra* 'forth', the verbal root √*kṛ* 'to do' and the feminine suffix *ti*, and it conveys the idea of 'bringing forth'. In the *Brahma-Vaivarta-Purāṇa* (II.1.5) these three morphemes are explained symbolically as representing *sattva*, *rajas* and *tamas* respectively.

Although the word itself does not occur prior to the metric Upaniṣads,[1] the concept of *prakṛti* appears to be known, in principle, already in the *Ṛgveda* and *Atharvaveda*. Citing F. O. Schrader (1955), K. B. R. Rao (1966, 99), for instance, conjectured that whilst the notion of *ātman* led to the formulation of the concept of *puruṣa*, the earlier concept of *brahman* as the substratum of the manifest world gave rise to the idea of *akṣara*, *avyakta* and, then, *prakṛti*. D. Chattopadhyaya (1959), again, proffered an entirely divergent view, linking up the evolution of this key concept with the fertility cult of what he regarded as the original non-vedic Sāṃkhya-Tantrism. 'Evidently the term *prakriti* was not the invention of the early Sankhya philosophers because it was the basic concept of Tantrism, the history of which is traced back to a very remote antiquity. And it is impossible to deny that the *prakriti* originally stood for the female principle without questioning the Indian cultural tradition fundamentally' (p. 404).

Despite the persuasiveness of D. Chattopadhyaya's tight-knit argumentation, I fail to be convinced by his sweeping reconstruction of the history of Indian thought and entertain certain reservations about his unilinear derivation of the philosophical concept of *prakṛti* from popular religious contexts. I have, however, similar misgivings about K. B. R. Rao's attempt to recognise in *Ṛgveda* I.164 and X.129 the earliest references to the proto-conception of *puruṣa* and *prakṛti*. I am not sure that he is justified in his conjecture that these two hymns must have 'in no small measure contributed to the breaking of the original absolutism of Brahman as the Personal *or* Impersonal into the dual Principles, the Personal *and* the Impersonal' (p. 114). It seems to me that the actual situation at the time must have been far more complex than is suggested by either view.

Besides, there are interesting references in the *Atharvaveda* which will have to be taken into account if one wants to arrive at a more comprehensive interpretation. Regrettably this whole hymnody has been rather neglected and underrated; possibly the fullest survey of the *Atharvaveda* from the viewpoint of proto-Yoga and -Sāṃkhya materials is that by J. W. Hauer (1922; 1927; 1958). For instance, he (1958, 59) saw in *Atharvaveda* X.8 a definite link with the much later *Śvetāśvatara-Upaniṣad*, which is one of the outstanding early Yoga texts,[2] and he also perceived in X.8.29–31 a clear indication of the germ of the later notion of *prakṛti*.

Of particular interest is here the use of the verbal root √*ac*/*añc* which J. W. Hauer regarded as the origin of the later concept of *vyakta* and *avyakta*. What seems to be the essence of these early expressions is the idea of a primal, transcendental source or 'womb' (*yoni*) from which issues the multiform universe. This is precisely the meaning of the concept of *prakṛti* as the creative matrix, the ἀρΧή, which holds *in posse* all things, itself being unbounded (ἄπειρον).

E. H. Johnston (1937), in his admirable and still useful study, has shown that the older term for *prakṛti* is *avyakta*, the 'unmanifest', still current at the time of the *Kaṭha-Upaniṣad* (fifth century B.C.?). In the *Bhagavad-Gītā*, which is slightly older than the *Śvetāśvatara-Upaniṣad*, but later than the *Kaṭha-Upaniṣad*, both terms are employed interchangeably. *Avyakta* is mentioned, for instance, in stanza VIII.18 and contrasted with the 'manifest' or *vyakta* (plural use), and in verse VIII.20 the word is employed to denote something which is higher than the ordinary *avyakta*; in the next verse this higher *avyakta* is identified with *akṣara*. At that time *prakṛti* had not yet acquired an exclusive technical sense (*viz*. 'nature'),[3] whereas *akṣara* (the 'imperishable'), signifying the principle of awareness, is decidedly a technical expression in the *Bhagavad-Gītā*.[4]

In the *Śvetāśvatara-Upaniṣad* (IV.10) the term *prakṛti* is found in the phrase *māyāṃ tu prakṛtiṃ vidyān māyinaṃ tu mahā-īśvaram*, '*prakṛti* is to be known as *māyā* [and] the great lord as the *māyin*'. Here *prakṛti* = *māyā* (not in the sense of 'illusion') stands for the unmanifest (*avyakta*) which elsewhere in the text is denoted by the word 'foundation' (*pradhāna*). E. H. Johnston (1937, 27) pointed out that since this particular stanza is in the *anuṣṭubh* metre it must have been inserted into this series of *triṣṭubh* verses at a later stage. The regular use of *prakṛti* for this period is in the plural, which refers to the set of eight primary evolutes, *viz. buddhi*, *ahaṃkāra*, *manas* and the five elements. This enumeration is according to the *Bhagavad-Gītā* (VII.4–5), but other variants are known.

For example, in the *Buddhacarita* (XII.18) these eight constituents are said to be *avyakta*, *buddhi*, *ahaṃkāra* and the five elements. This text also mentions the complementary set of sixteen *vikāras* or secondary evolutes, *viz.* the five senses, the five sense-objects, the five organs of action and the *manas* (see XII.19). This double usage of the term *prakṛti* is also retained in the *Sāṃkhya-Kārikā*, which speaks of *prakṛti* (in the later sense of *avyakta*) and of the various *prakṛtis* and *vikṛtis*, that is, the primary and secondary evolutes of the world-ground.

Remarkably, this is also the way in which Patañjali applies the term *prakṛti*. It is mentioned a mere three times in the *Yoga-Sūtra*, namely in I.19 as *prakṛti-laya* and in IV.2–3. In IV.3, significantly enough, the word is used in the plural genitive (as *prakṛtīnām*). The two *sūtras* in question run as follows: *jāty-antara-pariṇāmaḥ prakṛty-āpūrāt; nimittam-aprayojakaṃ prakṛtīnāṃ varaṇa-bhedas-tu tataḥ kṣetrikavat.* In consonance with J. W. Hauer's (1958) revised interpretation of the initial aphorisms of the fourth *pāda*, I suggest the following translation: 'The transformation into another category-of-existence (*jāti*) [derives] from the pouring-over of the world-ground. – The incidental-cause (*nimitta*) [*viz.* the store of subliminal-activators] does not initiate the *prakṛtis*, but [merely] singles out possibilities (*varaṇa*) [in accordance with the karmic conditions], like a farmer [who irrigates a field by selecting appropriate pathways for the water].'

The plural *prakṛtis* has been subjected to various renderings and paraphrases, such as 'evolving-causes' (J. H. Woods), 'Werdevorgänge' (J. W. Hauer), 'natural tendencies' (I. K. Taimni), 'die [schöpferisch sich betätigenden] Naturen' (P. Deussen), 'material causes' (G. Jha), 'creative-causes' (R. Prasāda) and 'constituents' (M. N. Dvivedi). Because of the classical commentators' complete misunderstanding of the true intent of these *sūtras*, which have nothing to do with magical feats, the obvious meaning of this plural use has never been spotted. Here we have not just a reference to some vaguely conceived process of creation, but very probably the plural *prakṛtis* refers to the well-known set of primary evolutes emerging from the primal matrix. Of course, one cannot be sure that Patañjali had in mind the set of eight principles as enunciated, for example, in the *Bhagavad-Gītā* or in other passages of the *Mahābhārata*. As a matter of fact his ontology – as will be seen – follows its own idiosyncratic pattern which is distinct from those promulgated in the epic, the *Caraka-Saṃhitā*, the *Buddhacarita* or other coeval sources.

Patañjali's vocabulary includes several synonyms of the term *prakṛti*. Thus he employs *dṛśya* (see II.17, 18, 21; IV.23), *grāhya* (I.41), *aliṅga* (I.45; II.19), and *sva* (II.23). E. H. Johnston (1937, 26) stated that *pradhāna* ('foundation') is the regular term used in the *Yoga-Sūtra*, but this word in fact occurs only once in III.48. The term *avyakta* ('unmanifest') on the other hand, does not appear at all. However, Patañjali employs *vyakta* (IV.13), contrasting it with *sūkṣma* ('the subtle'). These are said to be the two aspects of the *dharmas* ('constituents') which compose the universe; their essence are the primary-constituents or *guṇas*. In this instance *vyakta* and *sūkṣma* refer to the time dimension of things, *vyakta* being the generic term for those properties which are evident, *i.e.* present, and *sūkṣma* for those which are potential either because they existed in the past or will exist in the future.

The most common denotation for *prakṛti* is unquestioningly the term *dṛśya*, which covers both the unmanifest and the manifest aspects of *prakṛti*. This concept has an epistemological ring about it which is yet another indication of the psychological-experiential orientation of Yoga. Thus *dṛśya* (from √*dṛś* 'to see') signifies anything that is capable of becoming the object of the transcendental witness-Self, that is to say, anything that pertains to *prakṛti* in any of its modes, including the causal core (*pradhāna*) itself.

In this respect three major aspects of *prakṛti* can be differentiated: (i) the transcendental dimension, (ii) the objective (physical) part and (iii) the subjective (psychic) aspect. G. M. Koelman (1970, 158) called the last-mentioned, more appropriately perhaps, 'subjective-objective' by way of contrast with the 'objective-objective' energisations of *prakṛti*. The commentators appear to have taken *dṛśya* in a far more restricted sense. Thus the *Maṇiprabhā* (II.17) has *dṛśyaṃ buddhi-sattvam*, 'the seen is the translucent-aspect of the mind'. Vyāsa, again, says in his *Yoga-Bhāṣya* (II.17): *dṛśyā buddhi-sattva-upārūḍhāḥ sarve dharmāḥ*, 'The objects-of-sight (*dṛśyāḥ*) are all qualities [of *prakṛti*] which have affected the *sattva* of the mind'. Vācaspati Miśra explains this further in his *Tattva-Vaiśāradī* (II.17): *tad-etad-*

buddhi-sattvaṃ śabda-ādy-ākāravad-dṛśyam-ayas-kānta-maṇi-kalpaṃ puruṣasya svaṃ bhavati dṛśi-rūpasya svāminaḥ, 'Thus this same *sattva* of the mind, containing [the objects of] sound, etc., [becomes] the 'seen'; [acting] like a loadstone, it becomes the property (*sva*) of the Self, the proprietor of the form of Awareness'.

That Patañjali employs *dṛśya* in the widest possible sense is evident from aphorism II.18, where he delineates its main characteristics. He speaks of a 'disposition' (*śīla*) to (a) luminosity (*prakāśa*), (b) activity (*kriyā*) and (c) inertia (*sthiti*). This tripartition is the outcome of the presence of the three types of *guṇas*, as is apparent from *sūtra* II.19, which gives out the various levels of manifestation of these primary building-blocks of the world-ground. I will come back to this issue shortly.

I wish to conclude these pre-eminently linguistic observations by formalising them in the accompanying semantic matrix, constructed on the basis of the above synonyms of the term *prakṛti*.

	comprehensive concepts	restricted concepts
	sva	*prakṛti* (singular)
	dṛśya	*pradhāna*
PRAKṚTI	*grāhya*	*aliṅga*
		prakṛti (plural)
		vyakta – *sūkṣma*

It must next be asked what exactly *prakṛti* stands for. First of all, it is important to realise that it comprises two cardinal dimensions. On the one hand there is the noumenal matrix of creation, also called *aliṅga* (= *avyakta* = *pradhāna*), and on the other there is the realm of the multitudinous phenomena of contingent existence. The latter category is not exhausted by the visible universe of ordinary space and time. In its phenomenalised nature, *prakṛti* also embraces the vast hidden dimension impervious to the senses but experiencable in yogic introspection[5] and logically deducible from the spatio-temporal sense-derived data. This inner or 'subtle' (*sūkṣma*) aspect of *prakṛti* I propose to call *deep structure* in contradistinction to the *surface structure*, *i.e.* the visible, audible, tactual world.

The deep structure of *prakṛti* is stratified hierarchically, albeit in an aspatial sense. This stratification, which varies in its conception from one tradition to another, has also been referred to as 'ontological map', as it serves the *yogin* as a guide-beam in his programme of conscious involution.[6] Viewed dynamically rather than structurally, one can also speak of an evolution of ontic categories or *tattva-antara-pariṇāma*. The term *tattva* denotes such categories as *buddhi*, *ahaṃkāra*, etc.

This conception implies a view of the universe as an essentially autonomous system of necessarily interrelated events. This particular aspect of *prakṛti* was precipitated in the vedic concept of *ṛta* or 'order', and later on came to be expressed, for instance, in the idea of *adṛṣṭa* 'the invisible [law]' in the philosophy of Nyāya and Vaiśeṣika. *Prakṛti* can thus be looked upon as a system or 'field' composed of interdependent sub-systems arranged hierarchically according to the principle that each higher sub-system is progressively more inclusive. This is best illustrated on the example of the well-known schema utilised in Classical Sāṃkhya[7] which permits the accompanying diagrammatic condensation.

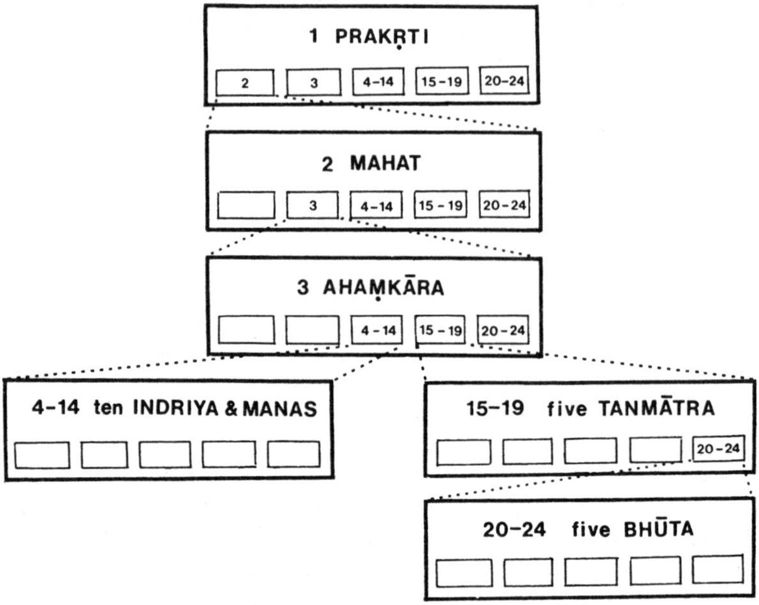

The co-ordination and interdependence between the several sub-systems are defined in terms of causal relation of a specific type. It is traditionally known as the 'doctrine of (pre-)existent effect' or *sat-kārya-vāda* or, more specifically, as the 'doctrine of (real) transformation' or *pariṇāma-vāda*. R. A. Sinari (1970, 38) styled this the 'earliest and epistemologically the most valuable attempt made in Indian philosophy to set up a theory of causal order'.

This view is partly foreshadowed in the *Bhagavad-Gītā* (II.16), which contains these lines: *na-asato vidyate bhāvo, na-abhāvo-vidyate sataḥ*, or 'Of the non-existent there is no becoming, of the existent there is no dis-becoming'. The full-fledged doctrine, being a restatement of the above notion, is to be found in the *Sāṃkhya-Kārikā* (9): *asad-akaraṇād-upādāna-grahaṇāt-sarva-saṃbhava-abhāvāt, śaktasya śakya-karaṇāt-kāraṇa-bhāvāc-ca sat-kāryam*, or '[There is] [pre-]existent effect because of the non-productivity of non-being, because of the need for a material-cause, because of the impossibility of derivation from everything, because of [a thing's] ability-to-produce [only what it is capable] of producing and because of the nature of the cause'.

This somewhat obscure passage stands in need of elucidation. The pre-existence of the effect in the cause is based on five logical arguments. The first is that something which does not exist in any mode of being whatsoever cannot be brought into existence, nor can it bring anything else into existence. This is the famous axiom *ex nihilo nihil fit*. The second reason adduced by Īśvara Kṛṣṇa is that any effect requires a cause which, in his opinion, must be of the same material. Next, it is argued that the effect must have a specific cause and cannot be derived simply from the sum total of other effects; there must be a special relation between effect and cause, and this is interpreted in the sense that the cause potentially contains the effect. Fourthly, not everything is capable of producing a specific effect, which is yet another affirmation of the essential inherence of the effect in the cause. Finally, the pre-existence of the effect in the cause is demanded by the fact that the cause is of the same nature as the effect.

These statements can hardly be said to amount to proofs unless a circular logic is thought admissible. Notwithstanding this criticism, it is interesting that Sāṃkhya and Yoga carefully distinguish between the material (*upādāna*) and the instrumental (*nimitta*) cause of a thing, subsuming both under the heading of *kāraṇa*, which is set against *kārya* or 'effect'. Occasionally the effect is defined as either *aupādānika* or *naimittika*.

All phenomena, whether they belong to the surface structure or to the deep structure of *prakṛti*, are considered as 'transformations' (*pariṇāma*) of one and the same substratum, *viz.* the world-ground. Here applies, if ever, the phrase *plus ça change, plus c'est la même chose.* The technical designation of this particular theorem is *prakṛti-pariṇāma-vāda*. It is one of four major theoretical positions on the issue of causality as developed in Indian philosophy.

There is first of all the view of the Nyāya and Vaiśeṣika schools of thought – known as *ārambha-vāda* – according to which eternal atoms create by continual re-combination the multiform universe. Also the Ājīvikas, Jainas and materialists of ancient India must be reckoned as subscribing to this view. The best known representative of the second type of interpretation is Hīnayāna Buddhism with its *dharma* theory. This *saṅghāta-vāda* asserts that separate existential factors create the individual and his external and internal environment by a process of co-operative collocation (*saṅghāta*). The third position is the *vivarta-vāda* which is characteristic of the non-dualism of Śaṅkara, according to which the one real *brahman* remains ever unchanged; all transformations are attributed to the contingent universe, which is regarded as *vivarta* or an appearance quite different in nature from its cause. The Mahāyāna thinkers maintain a similar view. Finally, the *pariṇāma-vāda* asserts that the Many is created out of the One by way of a series of real transformations, and it is this position which is typical of Yoga, Sāṃkhya and the older Vedānta schools.

The *pariṇāma-vāda* claimed a considerable following, and its prominent place in Indian philosophical speculation can readily be appreciated when one considers the frequent refutations of it by other traditions, especially Buddhism.[8] In later times Sāṃkhya and Yoga thinkers availed themselves also of such concepts as had been developed in opponent schools in order to buttress their position in the increasingly competitive world of analytical philosophising. For example, Patañjali adopts the concepts of quality (*dharma*) and substance (*dharmin*) which played a decisive role in the heyday of Indian philosophy.[9]

Intimately related to the concept of *prakṛti* is the doctrine of the *guṇas*, which I will discuss next. The world-ground as conceptualised in the Sāṃkhya and Yoga tradition has been described by some scholars as a kind of 'ultimate energy' transmuting itself into various conditions by means of a rearrangement of its basic constituents, the so-called *guṇas*, which invite comparison with the 'quantum packets' of modern nuclear physics.[10] The notion of the *guṇas* is one of the central doctrines of Yoga-Sāṃkhya ontology and can safely be regarded as the single most original contribution of this proliferating tradition.

The word *guṇa* means literally 'strand, rope' and is also used to denote 'quality'. In the present context it is perhaps best rendered as 'primary-constituent' of the world-ground. Other frequent translations are 'aspect' (J. H. Woods), 'quality' (S. Dasgupta), 'attribute' (G. Jha). N. Smart (1964) preferred to translate it as 'strand-substances' and J. W. Hauer (1958) as 'Weltstoff-Energien', whilst others retain the Sanskrit term (see I. K. Taimni, G. M. Koelman).

The doctrine of the *guṇas* has a protracted and rather recondite history. The idea was conceived long before the codification of either Yoga or Sāṃkhya, but its exact origins are shrouded in mystery. Various attempts have been made to trace the development of this important philosophical concept, with varying degrees of success.[11] The available historical data permit the conclusion that the *guṇa* theory was gradually developed out of much older speculations recorded in the vedic *saṃhitās*, the *brāmaṇa* texts and also the Upaniṣads.

There is no compelling reason to assume that the notion evolved within non-āryan traditions, though it may not have been the creation solely of the brāhmanic orthodoxy either. According to E. H. Johnston (1937), the *guṇas* were originally simply psychological qualities, and he referred to the use of the synonym *bhāva* or 'force of becoming, sentiment'. But as J. A. B. van Buitenen (1956) showed beyond all doubt, there are two types of evolutionary schemata advocated by Sāṃkhya, *viz.* a vertical and a horizontal theory of evolution which later on came to be integrated in some schools. He distinctly opposed the popular idea that the term *guṇa* (= *bhāva*) originally meant 'moral or psychical quality of the *buddhi*'. The original vertical version did not involve the *guṇas* at all. J. A. B. van Buitenen interpreted *bhāva* as a 'form of being, cosmic phase evolved under the influence of a *guṇa*'.[12]

Guṇa in its most archaic conception stood for a triad of factors one of which was *rajas*. Their combined action on *buddhi* resulted in the evolution of the three *bhāvas* or states of being which, according to J. A. B. van Buitenen's reconstruction of the epic evidence, probably consisted in *manas* (mind), the *indriyas* (senses) and the *bhūtas* (elements). The well-known triad of *sattva-rajas-tamas* is definitely a subsequent creation, though the principle implied in this conception must have been present already in the earlier triadic notion.

What then are the *guṇas* in their classical sense? Surprisingly enough this question has never been satisfactorily answered by any of the earlier thinkers, and it was in fact Vijñāna Bhikṣu who, as late as the sixteenth century, afforded this topic a first critical examination and discussion. The *guṇas* can be described as being the ultimate building-blocks of the material and mental phenomena in their entirety. They are not merely qualities or properties, but actual entities or 'reals' (S. Dasgupta, 1963[5]) and as such non-distinct from the world-ground itself.[13] They are the indivisible atoms of everything there is, with the exception of the Self (*puruṣa*), which is by definition *nir-guṇa*. The *guṇas* underlie every appearance, and are the world-ground in its noumenal character. This is expressed by Īśvara Kṛṣṇa in the following way: *tri-guṇam-aviveki viṣayaḥ sāmānyam-acetanaṃ prasava-dharmi, vyaktaṃ tatha pradhānaṃ tad-viparītas-tathā ca pumān*, or 'The manifest [world] and the primary-substratum [are both of the nature of] the triple *guṇas*, without discernment, objective, generic, without Awareness and productive. Yet the Self is the reverse of this.'[14]

Thus they are the very material of *prakṛti*. In fact in Classical Sāṃkhya *prakṛti* is defined as *tri-guṇa-sāmya-avasthā* or 'the state of homoeostasis of the three *guṇas*'.[15] In his study on the *Bhagavad-Gītā* S. Dasgupta (1965[4], II, 465) suggested that in this scripture the *guṇas* are not thought to constitute the world-ground, but this is obviously wrong, for he clearly overlooked stanza VII.14, where Kṛṣṇa's *māyā* (= *prakṛti*) is called *guṇa-mayī* or 'composed of the *guṇas*'. Nor do we need to perceive any real contradiction between this statement and such expressions as *guṇāḥ prakṛti-saṃbhavāḥ* (XIV.5) or 'the *guṇas* born of the world-ground'.

Any argument to the contrary would be meaningless in view of the *sat-kārya* doctrine which demands that the *guṇas* in their noumenal state are mere potentialities which becomes actualised with the process of evolution. As K. B. R. Rao (1966, 52) put it: '*Guṇas* are themselves *prakṛti*. *Guṇas* are not "ingredients", or "parts".' C. T. Kenghe (1958, 4) has a remark to the same effect: 'The three forces Sattva, Rajas and Tamas cannot be said to be the parts of Prakṛti, for in themselves they are equally impartite and impartite things can never be parts of anything else'. This author also called *prakṛti* a 'suprapsychical substance' rejecting the widely prevalent translation of the term with 'matter'; but this is equally obscure.

Patañjali is perfectly cogent on this issue. In aphorism II.19

aliṅga, which corresponds with the Sāṃkhya *prakṛti-pradhāna*, is said to be one of the levels (*parvan*) of the *guṇas*. There are four levels in all, which will be dealt with in detail below. Evidently, for all practical purposes, the *guṇas* can be equated with *prakṛti* (in the comprehensive sense).

The important question of the substantiality of the *guṇas* has been left untackled by both Vyāsa and Vācaspati Miśra, just as they ignored the problem of their multiplicity. The texts mention triple *guṇas* but do not explicitly state whether there are only three types of *guṇas* or a multitude of *guṇas* which may be classified into three categories in respect of their several functions. However, the postulation of a large number of *guṇas* seems a logical necessity if it is maintained that the plethora of phenomena are the direct outcome of infinite *guṇa* permutations, which is at least Īśvara Kṛṣṇa's proposition.

In his opinion the entire phenomenal world and its deep structure are created by a process of continual re-combination of the primary-constituents of *prakṛti*.[16] Indeed, if there were only three distinct entities the inordinate multiplicity of existing things could not be explained. On the other hand, it is convincing that a near infinite number of *guṇas* of three different types should, by way of collocation and perpetual re-combination, produce the multi-faceted dynamic network of existence.

Perhaps today this question can be resolved on a non-substantivist basis in the light of contemporary field theory, which has successfully supplanted the classical conception of matter as a chunk of substance floating in ampty space. Perhaps it is not too far-fetched to compare the *guṇas* with the atoms of modern nuclear physics, which are described as localisations of fields. As F. L. Kunz (1963, 5) put it: 'An atom [. . .] may be correctly thought of as a standing wave system in an open wave force field potential.' It is surely not by accident that it is always the energetic nature of the *guṇas* which is pushed into the foreground by expounders of the Sāṃkhya and Yoga traditions. Although Vijñāna Bhikṣu characterises them as *dravyas* or 'substances', he does so only in order to refute the Vaiśeṣika position according to which the *guṇas* are mere qualities. Had he known the expression 'energy parcel' he would presumably not have hesitated to use it instead.

As G. M. Koelman (1970, 77) noted, 'The *guṇas*' nature is throughout expressed in terms of functional qualities, kinetic dispositions and causal urges.' This is well illustrated by the *Yoga-Bhāṣya* (II.18). From this passage it emerges that

(1) although the *guṇas* are quite distinct entities having different characteristics,
(2) they nonetheless influence each other and by their interdependent functioning create the phenomenal universe, and thus
(3) everything must be looked upon as a 'synergisation'[17] of the three *guṇas*.

The energetic nature of the *guṇas* is furthermore borne out by the fact that Patañjali associates them with the concept of *pariṇāma* or 'transformation' and that of *pratiprasava* or 'involution', *i.e.* the flowing back of the manifest *guṇas* into the potentiality of the world-ground. Yoga ontology thus conceives Nature to be a quivering force field as it were undergoing continuous transformations. The dynamism is sustained by the incessant interaction of the three types of *guṇas* whose activity can be inferred from their phenotypes as experienced externally (in perception) or internally (in introspection).

The classic *guṇa* triad is headed by *sattva*. The word means literally 'being-ness' and is derived from *sat* 'being' and the abstract suffix *-tva*. A great variety of renderings have been proposed, such as 'intelligence-stuff' (S. Dasgupta), 'essentiality' (R. Prasāda), 'goodness' (G. Jha), all of which hardly touch the core meaning of this term. J. H. Woods (1966[3]) wisely left the word untranslated, but G. M. Koelman (1970, 10) contended that it is best rendered by its Latin equivalent *entia* (as in *presentia*, *absentia*), whilst the adjectival form *sāttvika* would correspondingly assume the appearance of 'entic'. I confess that I fail to see the advantage of such a procedure. If one has to have recourse to a foreign language anyhow in order to convey the meaning of *sattva*, might one not simply retain the Sanskrit term and maybe anglicise its adjective to sattvic?

The single most important study of the concept of *sattva* is that by J. A. B. van Buitenen (1957[b]), in which he finds fault with past scholarship for reading the classic expression of this concept into the older material. He noted: 'One result of this classicism was the acceptance of *sattva* and the other *guṇas* as factors only conditioning the individual's soul's *buddhi*, their cosmological function being looked upon either as secondary or as superseded' (p. 88). Thus J. A. B. van Buitenen completed the partial rectification of this aprioristic view by É. Senart (1915 and 1925).

In the pre-classical Sāṃkhya and Yoga traditions the term *sattva* was used in many different senses; it denoted the body-complex and also the psyche and the concretely existing entity or sentient being. J. A. B. van Buitenen (1957[b], 105) observed: 'It would seem that *sattva*, undoubtedly a notion that was elaborated in circles where the idea of a personality – with increasingly microcosmic features – persisted, reflects in its functions the aspect of *sat* as the reified and created. As such it could easily become linked up with tripartite creation . . .' He further remarked: 'It is not clear how *sattva* came to be associated just with *rajas* and *tamas*. Probably it succeeded to a principle like *tapas* or *jyotis*, which acquired the connotation of "light of knowledge" and had its opposite in "darkness" and "obscuration" ' (p. 106).

The second member of the *guṇa* triad is *rajas*, which according to J. A. B. van Buitenen probably 'brought the triadic pattern along' (p. 106). Like *sattva* this term has suffered various more or less adequate renderings into English, such as 'energy-stuff' (S. Dasgupta, F. V. Catalina), 'energy' (R. Prasāda), 'foulness' (G. Jha). É. Senart (1915), the first to afford this concept a thorough examination, showed that originally *rajas* signified the 'atmosphere'. This was challenged by T. Burrow (1948, 645), who related it to 'dirt' – 'moral defilement' ... 'cosmic principle'. However, this hypothetical reconstruction of the evolution of the concept of *rajas* was firmly rejected by J. A. B. van Buitenen (1957[b], 92), who was most insistent that *rajas* had, to begin with, a purely cosmological significance and that only subsequently did it acquire a microcosmic psychological meaning. To cover both the cosmic and the psychic aspect of this term, G. M. Koelman (1970, 12) used the Greek word *ἔργον*, paraphrasing *rajas* with 'ergetic constituent'. It is the active principle which stimulates, initiates action and supplies the dynamic impulses without which the field of *prakṛti* would collapse.

Finally, there is *tamas*, which has been translated as 'mass-stuff' (S. Dasgupta, F. V. Catalina), 'inertia' (R. Prasāda) and 'darkness' (G. Jha). Whilst *rajas* is derived from √*raj*/*rañj* 'to glow, be brilliant', *tamas* is a derivative of √*tam* 'to be exhausted, become rigid'. G. M. Koelman (1970, 12) connected it with the allied Latin term *temus* of which the ablative *temere* 'blindly, rashly' has survived. He called this third member of the *guṇa* triad accordingly the 'temeric constituent'.

S. Dasgupta (1963[5], I, 242–3) made an attempt to explain these *guṇas* as 'feeling-substances'. According to him, feelings 'mark the earliest track of consciousness, whether we look at it from the point of view of evolution or of the genesis of consciousness in ordinary life [. . .]. The feelings are therefore the things-in-themselves, the ultimate substances of which consciousness and gross matter are made up [. . .]. The three principal characteristics of thought and matter [. . .] are but the manifestations of three types of feeling substances.'

This seems to have been accepted *prima facie* by F. V. Catalina (1968, 35), but, interesting as S. Dasgupta's perspective is, it nevertheless implies an unwarranted psychologisation of the nature of the *guṇas*. Such a one-sidedness must be avoided if one wants to do full justice to this complex concept. The *guṇas* are both cosmogonic and psychogonic forces. This ambivalent nature of the primary-constituents is indeed confusing, accustomed as we are to distinguish carefully between material phenomena on the one hand and psychomental events on the other hand. But, again, we must take heed not to project our own cognitive patterns onto the Indian schemata.

One can sympathise with R. Garbe (1917[2], 272), who styled the doctrine of the *guṇas* a 'strange theory', but he was decidedly mistaken in his further statement that it is 'a pure hypothesis [. . .] which shares the fate with many other philosophical hypotheses not to be able to hold good in the light of modern natural science' (p. 284). On the contrary, this striking teaching is far from being merely a weird product of early man's vivid imagination. It seems a reasonably cogent framework of explanation of reality as encountered by the trained *yogin*.

Like the concept of *prakṛti*, that of the *guṇas*, too, cannot be regarded as based on mere fiction. Rather more compelling is the unpopular view that these are experientially derived concepts. To gainsay this *a priori* is to deny the *raison d'être* of Yoga and of the older Sāṃkhya which are geared for experience rather than abstract speculation. Little wonder that S. Radhakrishnan (1951[6], II, 274), apparently oblivious to this explanation, was constrained to make the following admission: 'It is difficult to understand the precise significance of the Sāṃkhya account of evolution, and we have not seen any satisfactory explanation as to why the different steps of evolution are what they are. – The different principles of the Sāṃkhya system cannot be logically deduced from *prakṛti*, and they seem to be set down as its products, thanks to historical accidents. There is no deductive development of the products from the one *prakṛti*. Vijñāna-bhikṣu is aware of this defect, and so asks us to accept the Sāṃkhya account of evolution on the authority of the scriptures. But this is to surrender the possibility of philosophical explanation.'

In rejecting Vijñāna Bhikṣu's answer, S. Radhakrishnan simultaneously forfeited the only reasonable explanation of these concepts which embody experiential knowledge. For what is the foundation of the authority of the scriptures if not 'revelation' in the sense of the experience of reality in non-ordinary states of consciousness (such as meditation or *samādhi*)? Admittedly, such an interpretation is seemingly contradicted by the fact that all these concepts have a history, that is, underwent a process of development and did not just spring into existence ready-made and *ex nihilo*.

However, gradual conceptual refinement is an integral part of the life of any theory, and this fact by no means undermines the data themselves, which, in this particular case, are the subjective 'observations' during meditative and enstatic states of consciousness. The question is rather to what degree the later doctrinal sophistications, especially those of Classical Sāṃkhya, can be said to do justice to the original experiences.

But to come back to the word *guṇa*, we find that it is used altogether six times in the *Yoga-Sūtra* (*viz.* I.16; II.15, 19; IV.13, 32, 34). To these instances must be added *sūtra* II.18, which mentions the phenotypes (*śīla*) of the three *guṇas*, namely *prakāśa*[18] or 'luminosity' (pertaining to *sattva*), *kriyā* or 'activity' (belonging to *rajas*) and *sthiti* or 'inertia' (connected with *tamas*). K. B. R. Rao (1966, 54), who was bold enough to speak of 'the scientific character of the theory of *guṇas*' (p. 51), epitomised their respective nature as follows: *Sattva* is that 'which makes for existence or beingness'; *rajas* is that 'which makes for change in itself', and *tamas* is that 'which denies annihilation through change'. In other words, *sattva* represents the principle of existence, *rajas* that of discontinuity and *tamas* that of continuity.

These are said (II.18) to be 'bodied forth' in the elements and the senses. The exact Sanskrit phrase is *bhūta-indriya-ātmakam*, which J. H. Woods (1966[3]) rendered as 'with the elements and organs as its essence'. R. Prasāda (1912) has 'it consists of the elements and the powers of sensation', whilst J. W. Hauer (1958) is in agreement with the above interpretation ('körpert sich dar in Elementen und Organen').

Of course, these elements and senses as the external aspects of the *guṇas* merely constitute what I have previously called the 'surface structure' of *prakṛti*. To express the same idea, Patañjali employs the technical term *viśeṣa* or 'the particularised' (see II.19). The 'deep structure' of the gargantuan body of *prakṛti*, on the other hand, is stratified into three primary levels of increasing complexity and organisation; these are the so-called *guṇa-parvans* or 'levels of the *guṇas*', namely *aviśeṣa* ('the unparticularised'), *liṅga-mātra* ('the differentiated') and *aliṅga* ('the undifferentiate'), which is the most generic stratum.

According to M. N. Dvivedī (1934[3]) these *parvans* are identical with the 'four stages' allegedly described in I.45; but this particular aphorism does not mention any stages at all, and he himself quite correctly translated *sūkṣma-viṣayatvaṃ ca-aliṅga-paryavasānam* as 'The province of the subtle ends with the indissoluble'. I. K. Taimni (1965[2], 180), again, attempted to correlate the levels of the *guṇas* with the stages of *samādhi* mentioned in I.17 and also with the vedāntic notion of the *kośas* or 'sheaths'. He proposed the following equations:

vitarka-samādhi	—	*viśeṣa*	—	*manomaya-kośa*
vicāra-°	—	*aviśeṣa*	—	*vijñānamaya-*°
ānanda-°	—	*liṅga*	—	*ānandamaya-*°
asmitā-°	—	*aliṅga*	—	*ātman*

The apparent neatness of this tabulation is matched only by its total fictitiousness. First of all, it is misleading to equate the enstatic experience of the undifferentiate (*aliṅga*) with the realisation of *ātman* in Vedānta. The latter is on a par with the yogic *puruṣa* as the principle of Awareness, whereas *aliṅga* is without question conceived of as an insentient category. If a comparison can be made at all, one would rather expect that it is the 'sheath made of bliss' (*ānandamaya-kośa*) which corresponds with the undifferentiate, as both are regarded as the root of spiritual nescience. The 'sheath made of consciousness' (*vijñānamaya-kośa*), again, would seem to be more properly related to *buddhi* as the higher mental faculty, and the 'sheath made of mentation' (*manomaya-kośa*) could then be made to run parallel to the mind (*manas*) and the sensory complex. The realm of the particularised (*viśeṣa*) entails also the five coarse elements (*sthūla-bhūta*) which, if one wanted to be consistent, would call for the inclusion of the fifth and lowest (or outermost) 'sheath' as well, namely the 'sheath made of food' (*annamaya-kośa*). Thus one would have to squeeze a pentadic classificatory system (*i.e.* the *pañca-kośa* doctrine) into a quaternary schema (*i.e.* the *parvan* doctrine), which is unsatisfactory and in this particular case misleading as well.

I. K. Taimni's second contention according to which there is a correlation between the four types of enstasy (*samādhi*) and the *guṇa-parvans* is at first sight more promising, but on closer examination it reveals itself to be equally fallacious. For the cogitative enstasy (*vitarka-samādhi*) concerns only the coarse (*sthūla*) aspect of *prakṛti*, that is, the manifold composites of the five categories of elements (*bhūta*) existing in the space-time universe. On the other hand, the reflexive enstasy (*vicāra-samādhi*) relates to all subtle entities up to the undifferentiate (*aliṅga*, see I.45), that is, the entire deep structure of *prakṛti*. The beatific enstasy (*ānanda-samādhi*), again, is directed towards the instruments of knowledge (*i.e.* the senses) if we can rely on the testimony of the commentators, whilst the *asmitā-samādhi* is orientated towards the principle of individuality (*asmitā*).

Nor must one confuse the four 'levels' on which the *guṇas* manifest themselves with the ontogenetic series. It appears that Patañjali's four-level model is a structural view of the universe constituted by the primary-constituents (*guṇa*) and is not meant to explain the actual evolutionary process in which the individual ontic categories (*tattva*) emerge from the world-ground. In fact Patañjali does not refer to the *tattva* evolution at all and merely mentions some of the emergent categories of existence, such as the elements, the senses and the mind. The term *buddhi* appears to be used in the sense of 'cognition' only. *Ahaṃkāra* (lit. 'I-maker') is probably replaced by *asmitā* (lit. 'I-amness'), and, significantly, the *tanmātras*[19] are nowhere mentioned.

The crucial problem now is one of assigning the ontic categories to Patañjali's four-level model. Vyāsa (II.19) advances this correlated schema:

tatra-ākāśa-vāyv-agny-bhūmayo bhūtāni śabda-sparśa-rūpa-rasa-gandha-tanmātrāṇām-aviśeṣānāṃ viśeṣāḥ, tathā śrotra-tvak-cakṣu-jihvā-ghrāṇāni buddhi-indriyāṇi, vāk-pāṇi-pāda-pāyu-upasthāni karma-indriyāṇi, ekādaśaṃ manaḥ sarva-artham, ity-etāny-asmitā-lakṣaṇasya-aviśeṣasya viśeṣāḥ, guṇānām-eṣa ṣoḍaśako viśeṣa-pariṇāmaḥ, ṣaḍ-aviśeṣāḥ, tad-yathā śabda-tanmātraṃ sparśa-tanmātram rūpa-tanmātraṃ raṣa-tanmātraṃ gandha-tanmātrañ-ca, ity-eka-dvi-tri-catuṣ-pañca-lakṣaṇāḥ śabda-ādayaḥ pañca-aviśeṣāḥ, ṣaṣṭaś-ca-aviśeṣo'smitāmātra iti, ete sattāmātrasya-ātmano mahataḥ ṣaḍ-aviśeṣa-pariṇamaḥ, yat tat-param-aviśeṣebhyo liṅgamātraṃ mahat-tattvam.

I submit the following translation:

Of this [four-level structure] the elements 'ether', 'air', 'fire' and 'earth' are the particularised [modifications] of the unparticularised potentials (*tanmātra*), [*viz.*] sound, touch, form-percept (*rūpa*), taste and smell. Similarly, ear, skin, eye, tongue and nose are the cognitive organs, [whilst] voice, hands, feet, anus and genitals are the conative organs. The eleventh [particularised modification] is the multi-objective (*sarva-artha*) mind. These are the particularised (*viśeṣa*) [modifications] of the unparticularised, [which is] characterised as I-am-ness (*asmitā*). This is the sixteenfold particularised modification of the *guṇas*. The unparticularised [modifications] are six; they are the sound-potential, the touch-potential, the sight-potential (*rūpa-tanmātra*), the taste-potential and the smell-potential. Thus sound, etc., [having respectively] one, two, three, four or five characteristics, [add up to] five unparticularised [modifications]. And the sixth unparticularised [modification] is the 'substratum-of-I-am-ness' (*asmitā-mātra*). These are the six unparticularised modifications (*aviśeṣa-pariṇāma*) of the great entity, the 'substratum-of-beingness' (*sattā-mātra*). That which is superior to the unparticularised [modifications] is the 'substratum-of-[all that bears]-characteristics' (*liṅga-mātra*), the great principle.

Whether or not this exegesis is trustworthy cannot definitely be ascertained. However, it is quite remarkable that Vyāsa here makes ample use of Patañjali's own specific terminology, while elsewhere often completely ignoring it and superimposing his personal nomenclature on that of the *Yoga-Sūtra*. The above excerpt from the *Yoga-Bhāṣya* can be reduced to the following diagram, which shows up Vyāsa's correlation of the four ontic levels (*parvan*) with the better known series of *tattvas*:

aliṅga (the undifferentiate)
↓
liṅga-mātra (the differentiate)
↓
aviśeṣa (the unparticularised) = *asmitā-mātra* + the five *tanmātras* (potentials)
↓
viśeṣa (the particularised) = *manas* (mind) + the ten *indriyas* (senses) + the five *bhūtas* (elements)

I will next analyse each of the four *parvans* separately. To begin with the concept of *aliṅga*, the word itself is composed of the negative prefix *a-* and *liṅga* (from √*liṅg*/*lag* 'to attach, adhere, cling to') and has the meaning of 'that which is without mark or sign', in the following rendered as 'the undifferentiate'. *Aliṅga* is first used in the metric Upaniṣads, where it designates the Self.[20] However, in the *Yoga-Sūtra* it is clearly a synonym of *prakṛti* in its noumenal state as the matrix of the evolved cosmos.

As such *aliṅga* corresponds with the Sāṃkhya concept of *avyakta* or 'the unmanifest'. G. M. Koelman (1970, 88) described it as the 'non-resoluble genetic entity', apparently having in mind the traditional interpretation of the term *liṅga* as 'the mergent', that is, that which resolves into the world-ground upon the accomplishment of emancipation.[21] However, this interpretation of *aliṅga* is of secondary importance only. Its primary connotation is 'the signless' or, less accurately, 'the sexless'.[22] Hence I reject J. H. Wood's (1966[3], 91) translation of the term with 'unresoluble-primary-matter'.

From the ultimate substrative cause – *aliṅga* (*natura naturans*) – derives the first of the series of ontic evolutes (*natura naturata*), namely *liṅga-mātra* or 'the differentiated'. The second half of this interesting compound, *mātra*, is customarily employed in the sense of 'only, mere', but in the present philosophical context it must be credited with a more substantial meaning. In its oldest usage *mātrā* signified as much as 'substance' or 'material',[23] and the later form *mātra* as met with in such compounds as *liṅga-mātra*, *asmitā-mātra* or *tan-mātra* has unquestionably retained a shade of the original meaning. Hence in the above-quoted passage from the *Yoga-Bhāṣya* (II.19) I have risked translating it tentatively as 'substratum-of-°'.

But what does the concept of *liṅga-mātra* stand for? Even though there is no definition of this term in the *Yoga-Sūtra*, and in fact the word occurs but once (in II.19), its meaning can be fairly reliably inferred from the context and from the additional evidence of comparable ontological models. Vyāsa quite rightly identifies it as 'the great principle' (*mahat-tattva*) or 'mere being-ness' (*sattā-mātra*). As the direct source of all further differentiations of the undifferentiate noumenal world-ground, *liṅga-mātra* itself has but a single characteristic, which is 'existence'. Little more can be predicated of it than that it exists; it is non-differentiated existence.

In G. M. Koelman's (1970, 92) words, 'This state of "being-only" is not a state of functional activity, whereby it could be characterized [. . .]. It is the level of pure non-functional existence. The only operation it may be said to possess is its self-differentiation into the following evolutes. But this is a cosmical energization, but a functional activity.' In other traditions this threshold from the noumenal to the phenomenal is known as 'the golden germ' (*hiraṇya-garbha*) or as 'the lord of creatures' (*prajāpati*), and it can be compared with the νοῦς in the philosophy of Neoplatonism.

According to S. Dasgupta (1920, 51) the term *liṅga-mātra* is a synonym of *asmitā-mātra* (as used in IV.4), but this is an unfounded assumption which is not corroborated by the evidence in the *Yoga-Sūtra* itself or in any of the scholia. J. W. Hauer (1958, 286), generally displaying a more critical acumen than his predecessors, unexpectedly committed the same blunder, only to contradict and thus unwittingly correct himself on p. 288 of the same work. Nor must *liṅga-mātra* be equated with *buddhi*,[24] which, in Patañjali's philosophical jargon, stands for 'cognition' only and not for any ontological entity.

The third level (*parvan*) of the primary-constituents is known as *aviśeṣa* or 'the unparticularised' (from √*śiṣ* 'to leave'). The word is used only twice in the *Yoga-Sūtra*, once in the general sense of 'not distinguished' (III.35) and then in the strictly technical sense (II.19). Again, Patañjali offers no definition of this important concept. According to Vyāsa it is an umbrella term covering *asmitā-mātra* and the set of five *tanmātras*. This is a plausible enough explanation, but there is no degree of certainty about whether or not Patañjali actually included the concept of *tanmātra* in his ontogenetic model. In view of the fact that virtually all ancient and modern commentators insist on the inclusion of the *tanmātras*, I will briefly delineate their essential nature.

The word *tanmātra* (lit. 'that only') is, like most of these concepts, difficult to translate. Various suggestions have been made, such as 'fine element' (J. H. Woods), 'rudimentary element' (G. Jha), 'sensation' (I. K. Taimni), 'subtle element' (G. J. Larson), 'Grundstoff' (R. Garbe) and 'Subtilenergie' (J. W. Hauer). Possibly S. Dasgupta's rendering of the term with 'potential' best captures its meaning: 'The tanmātras possess something more than quantum of mass and energy; they possess physical characters, some of them penetrability, others powers of impact or pressure, others radiant heat, others again capability of viscous and cohesive attraction.'[25] This interpretation is based on B. N. Seal (1915), who defined the *tanmātras* as energy potentials, being the essences of the sensory faculties. However, this does not resolve any of the obscurity which surrounds this conception, and with G. J. Larson (1969, 205) one is forced to admit that '[e]xactly what is meant by "subtle element" is difficult if not impossible to determine'.

G. J. Larson also drew attention to the *Sāṃkhya-Kārikā* (38), which describes the *tanmātras* as *aviśeṣa*, thus opposing them to the elements (*bhūta*) which are said to be *viśeṣa*. This appears to be essentially the application of both terms in the *Yoga-Sūtra* as well. Vyāsa proffers this explanation: there are six 'unparticularised' modifications of the primary substratum, the sixth being *asmitā-mātra* (which is excluded in Īśvara Kṛṣṇa's version). He arranges them in the following manner:

(1) *śabda-tanmātra* — potential of sound
(2) *sparśa-°* — potential of touch
(3) *rūpa-°* — potential of sight (lit. 'form')
(4) *rasa-°* — potential of taste
(5) *gandha-°* — potential of smell
(6) *asmitā-mātra* — substratum of I-am-ness

No definitions are supplied by the author of the *Yoga-Bhāṣya*, but he makes mention of the fact that they are to be distinguished by their respective number of characteristics, which may be one, two, three, four or five. Vācaspati Miśra furnishes the requisite attributions:

(1) *śabda-tanmātra* — one characteristic only
(2) *sparśa-°* — two characteristics
(3) *rūpa-°* — three characteristics
(4) *rasa-°* — four characteristics
(5) *gandha-°* — five characteristics.

The number of characteristics inherent in each *tanmātra* is explained by the number of ways in which the corresponding element (*bhūta*) can be experienced. Each subsequent element incorporates the properties of all the previous elements. Thus while the ether (*ākāśa*) pertaining to *śabda-tanmātra* can only be heard, the air (*vāyu*) pertaining to *sparśa-tanmātra* can be heard and felt; fire (*agni*) can be heard, felt and seen, hence its corresponding *tanmātra*, which is *rūpa-°*, is stated to have three characteristics; water (*udaka*) can be heard, felt, seen and tasted and consequently its matrix, which is *rasa-tanmātra*, is said to display four characteristics; finally, earth (*bhūmi*) can be heard, felt, seen, tasted and smelled, wherefore *gandha-tanmātra* must have five characteristics.[26]

These *tanmātras* are, as G. M. Koelman (1970, 114) put it, 'objective universals', which do not stand for any particular sound, taste or visual percept but are sound as such, taste as such. Moreover, he made the valuable observation that they are not purely logical categories, but unlike the *objectum formale* of Scholasticism are experiencable ontic reals; however, as they are prior to sensation they can only be experienced by way of immediate apperception as cultivated by the *yogin*. We merely recognise their effects in the properties of their material counterparts, the elements.

Whether or not Patañjali operated with the *tanmātra* concept, *asmitā-mātra* must definitely be assigned to the *aviśeṣa* category. Whereas *liṅga-mātra* is a category (*tattva*) of which nothing can be predicated save that it exists, *asmitā-mātra* 'differentiates and pluralizes the indetermined and universal principle of being (*sattāmātra*) into so many different centres of reference, so many sources of initiative'.[27] And (*ibid.*): 'These centres of reference constitute, so to say, distinct nucleations within the one *Prakṛti*, in such a way that there arise different suppositions or subjectivations, or numerically distinct units of centralization, adapted to the needs of each particularized Self. This suppositation is sufficiently stable to be called a substantial entity, a *tattva* or a *dravya*.' *Asmitā-mātra* is, in other words, that agency which splits the primary substratum into subjects *vis à vis* objects in the form of a bifurcate line of evolution.

This concept corresponds with the Sāṃkhya notion of *ahaṃkāra*, described by A. Kunst (1968, 273) as 'a sort of ego-factory'. The author of the *Yuktidīpikā* (on *Sāṃkhya-Kārikā* 4) is therefore mistaken in maintaining that Patañjali does not know *ahaṃkāra* as a separate entity but includes it in *mahat*.[28] Similarly erroneous is S. Radhakrishnan's statement that Yoga 'does not recognise ahaṃkāra and manas as separate from buddhi'.[29]

This confusion could have been avoided by acknowledging the fact that Patañjali's vocabulary is not merely a replica of Sāṃkhya terminology. *Asmitā-mātra* is to him the 'universal' principle of individualisation (corresponding with *mahat* of the *Yuktidīpikā*), whereas *asmitā* denotes the particularised 'I-am-ness'. Thus a distinction is made between the ontological (structural) and the psychological (functional) use of this important term. *Asmitā-mātra* occurs only in IV.4, where it is unequivocally designated as the source of the multiple individualised minds or *nirmāṇa-cittas*. On the other hand, *asmitā* as a function of the phenomenal mind is mentioned in II.3, 6 and III.47, and in I.17 as a particular variable of cognitive enstasy (*samādhi*).

Of special interest is Patañjali's use of *asmitā-mātra*, the pre-individualised ontic reality of subjectivity. The introduction of this special technical designation does away with much of the ambiguity connected with the older term *ahaṃkāra*,[30] which is employed both in the sense of 'individualised ego-consciousness' and as 'pre-individualised generic principle of egohood'. Most commentators ignore the second connotation of *ahaṃkāra*, which induced J. A. B. van Buitenen

(1957[a]) to dedicate considerable space to this concept in order to correct the past lopsided interpretations and to bring out the 'I-maker's' 'cosmic function of creator of the empirical universe' (p. 15). His penetrating analysis is of relevance also to the study of the concept of *asmitā-mātra* in Classical Yoga.

J. A. B. van Buitenen pointed out the mythological elements present in the notion of *ahaṃkāra* and made it clear that 'the origin of the creative *ahaṃkāra* must be sought in the ancient upaniṣadic speculations on a self-formulating, self-creating primordial personality' (p. 21). He criticised the current exclusive interpretation of the term as that organ which forms the conception of the ego, putting forward the idea that 'if this had been the intended meaning when the term was coined, one wonders why the responsible thinker, capable of such conceptual thought, did not express himself more accurately in *ahaṃtā-kāra*. Besides, °*kāra* has as a rule the much more concrete sense of "fashioning, building, making and doing with one's hands" ' (p. 16).

He observed further: 'Side by side with *ahaṃkāra* we find in later texts *mamakāra*. Explications of *ahaṃkāra* take always the form of a quoted sentence with *iti*: "I am . . . I do . . ." etc.; of *mamakāra*: "This is mine" etc. This points to another meaning of °*kāra*, not as in *kumbhakāra* etc., but as in *oṃkāra*, *vaṣaṭkāra*, *svāhākāra*, etc.: "the cry, uttering or ejaculation: *Aham!*" ' (p. 17).

It is this creative aspect of *ahaṃkāra*, as anticipated in the words *ahaṃ bahu syam* ('May I be many') of the *Chāndogya-Upaniṣad* (VI.2.3), which is crystallised in the concept of *asmitā-mātra*. Although Patañjali merely asserts that the *nirmāṇa-cittas* originate from *asmitā-mātra*, it is safe to assume that *asmitā-mātra* also acts as the source of the *tanmātras* (granted that they are a part of Patañjali's ontology) and the elements (*bhūta*) and senses (*indriya*). This successive evolution can be depicted graphically as shown.

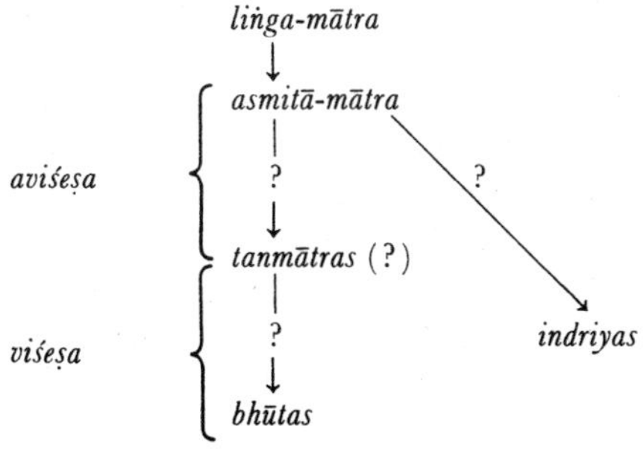

Vācaspati Miśra, for no apparent reasons, places *asmitā-mātra* and the *tanmātras* on the same ontogenetic level in as much as he regards both as evolutes of *buddhi* (= *liṅga-mātra*).[31] However, both on logical and on historical grounds the vertical derivation suggested above makes more sense. As G. M. Koelman (1970, 115) noted, 'Since the functions of cognition are evolved from the Ego-function, it seems plausible that the objective universals are evolved from the same Ego-function; this seems even more probable when we consider that the pure Ego-function on the existential level (*asmitā-mātra*) is also the prakritic subject of the activity of cognizing.'

This brings us to the last *guṇa-parvan*, the level of the particularised phenomena or *viśeṣa*, that is, the 'surface structure' of *prakṛti*. Contrary to Īśvara Kṛṣṇa, the author of the *Yoga-Sūtra* does not equate *aviśeṣa* solely with the *tanmātras* and *viśeṣa* with the *bhūtas* but includes in the category of *viśeṣa* also the *indriyas*.[32] This is hinted at by the phrase *bhūta-indriya-ātmaka* (II.18) and possibly also by the compound *kāya-indriya* (II.45).

The word *indriya* occurs seven times in the *Yoga-Sūtra*: II.18 (*bhūta-indriya*), II.41 (*indriya-jaya*), II.43 (*kāya-indriya*), II.54 (*indriyāṇāṃ pratyāhāra*), II.55 (*vaśyatā indriyāṇām*), III.13 (*bhūta-indriya*), and III.47 (*indriya-jaya*). *Indriya* is an old term, already well known to the composers of the early Upaniṣads. As a distinct ontogenetic set the *indriyas* are first mentioned in the *Kaṭha-Upaniṣad* (III.3–4) in the famous allegory of the chariot (= body) which is spun to horses (= senses) by means of reins (= mind) held by the chariot-driver (= *buddhi*).

The *Bṛhadāraṇyaka-Upaniṣad* contains an archaic passage – III.2.1–9 – in which we find one of the earliest analyses of the sensory tools. An interesting distinction is made between the eight 'graspers' (*graha*) and their corresponding 'super-graspers' (*ati-graha*):

(1) The in-breath (*prāṇa*) is 'supergrasped' by the out-breath (*apāna*).
(2) Speech (*vāc*) is 'supergrasped' by name (*nāma*).
(3) The tongue (*jihvā*) is 'supergrasped' by taste (*rasa*).
(4) The eye (*cakṣus*) is 'supergrasped' by form (*rūpa*).
(5) The ear (*śrotra*) is 'supergrasped' by sound (*śabda*).
(6) The mind (*manas*) is 'supergrasped' by desire (*kāma*).
(7) The hands (*hasta*) are 'supergrasped' by action (*karman*).
(8) The skin (*tvac*) is 'supergrasped' by touch (*sparśa*).

In later times this somewhat random enumeration came to be replaced by the classical double set of five conative and five cognitive senses, known as the *karma-indriyas* and the *jñāna-* or *buddhi-indriyas* respectively. To these must be added the mind or *manas* as the relay station for all other sensory capacities. Its inclusion among the *indriyas* brings to the fore one all-important point, namely that, correctly speaking, these *indriyas* must not be confused with the sense organs themselves, but they represent their intrinsic capacities. This was recognised long ago by R. Garbe (1917^2, 320): 'These ten senses must not be mixed up with the visible organs (*goloka*) in which they have their seat (*adhiṣṭhana*); they are in fact supra-sensory (*atīndriya*) and can only be deduced from their functions.' However, his words have been heeded by very few translators.[33]

Manas is used thrice in the *Yoga-Sūtra* (III.48; I.35; II.35) and very probably has the usual denotation as that mental capacity which organises the sensory input, or as K. B. R. Rao (1966, 68) put it, 'the synthesising factor of the experience got by the *indriyas*' which 'converts the indeterminate percepts into a determinate idea'. It is a moot point whether *manas* should be assigned to the *aviśeṣa* category, or whether Patañjali conceived of it as just another *indriya* pertaining to the *viśeṣa* category. Vyāsa, as we have seen, favours the latter solution.

Turning next to the set of five elements which together with the senses compose the *viśeṣa-parvan*, we find that Patañjali employs the term *bhūta* five times, *viz.* once in the sense of 'creature' (III.17), once as a participle (III.20: *aviṣayī-bhūtatvāt*) and thrice in the sense of 'element' (II.18; III.13, 44). Although the elements – ether, air, fire, water and earth – are not individually listed, Patañjali was undoubtedly acquainted with the *bhūtas* as ontogenetic factors. They belong to the classic stock of Yoga-Sāṃkhya metaphysics.

In passing, it may be remarked that the *Yoga-Sūtra* contains no reference to the 'atoms' (*aṇu*) as the ultimate subdivisions of the elements, and the statements of the commentators must be taken *cum grano salis*. The word *aṇimān* 'fineness', denoting the yogic paranormal ability to miniaturise the body (see III.45),[34] does not necessarily imply that Patañjali subscribed to the atomic theory as developed in the Vaiśeṣika school. The unmodified adoption of Kaṇāda's atomic theory would be difficult to reconcile with Patañjali's *guṇa* theory, which is meant to explain much the same phenomena. Besides, the word already appears in the *Chāndogya-Upaniṣad*

(VI.6; 8) at a time when the notion of atoms was certainly not yet formulated.

It should now be possible to attempt an overall reconstruction of Patañjali's implicit ontogenetic model on the basis of the information gleaned from the *Yoga-Sūtra* and comparable sources. The findings presented on the preceding pages can be epitomised in the accompanying diagram. Granted that this conjectural model is correct,

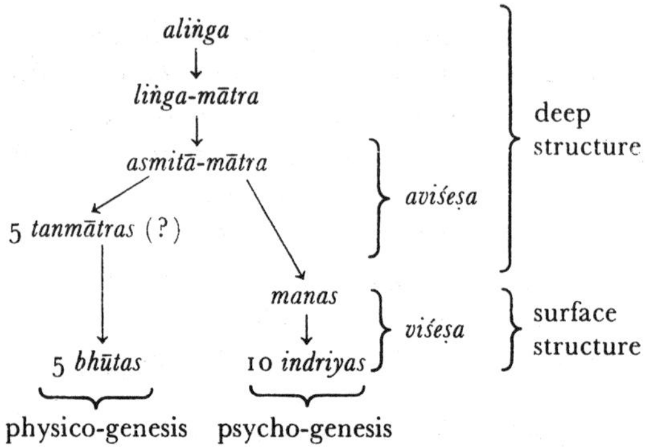

Patañjali apparently favoured a version of ontogenesis which has been grossly distorted by the classical exegetes. Furthermore, the present reconstruction discredits all those misinformed efforts which reduce the ontology of Classical Yoga to that of Classical Sāṃkhya. On the other hand, it is equally incorrect to assert, as did J. W. Hauer (1958, 282), that Patañjali made no use of ontogenetic categories at all but rather subsumed everything under the generic heading of *citta*, as derived from *asmitā-mātra*. I will substantiate this particular criticism in a subsequent chapter (see pp. 58 ff).

IV
The Concept of Emancipation

In view of the preceding reappraisal of the ontology of Classical Yoga which led to multiple corrections of long-standing misconceptions about it, it seems desirable to re-examine also the concept of emancipation (*apavarga*), 'the greatest original contribution of Indian philosophy'.[1] For if *īśvara* and *puruṣa* must, as I have tried to demonstrate, be understood differently from what has commonly been assumed ever since Vyāsa superimposed the views of his particular school on the philosophy of Patañjali, this can be expected to have its logical reverberations necessarily also in the conception of the ultimate concern of Yoga.

The recognised designation for this concept is *kaivalya*, which can be said to be a yogic term *par excellence*. Its earliest known occurrence is in fact in the *Yoga-Sūtra*, where it is employed in II.25, III.50, III.55 and IV.26. *Kaivalya* is the guṇated form of *kevala*, meaning 'alone' or, more significantly, 'the alone' (*i.e.* the Self).[2] The latter word is frequently used in the *Mahābhārata*, and in the philosophical sense occurs, for instance, in XII.294.43; 296.13, 29; 304.16, 26; 306.5, 74, 77, 79. The *Śvetāśvatara-Upaniṣad* (I.11; IV.18) also knows this usage.

In the *Maitrāyaṇīya-Upaniṣad* (IV.21) the term *kevalatva* or 'aloneness' is introduced, though it is doubtful whether this particular section belongs to the oldest material of the text.[3] Finally, as H. Zimmer (1953², 305 f.) pointed out, the words *kevala* and *kaivalya* also played a significant role in the philosophy of older Jainism. The word *kevala* is found, for instance, in the *Tattvārthādhigama-Sūtra* (I.9, 30; X.1), and in aphorism VIII.8 of the same text occurs the compound *kevala-darśana* in the sense of 'absolute intuition'. Moreover, the great pathfinders of Jainism, the *tīrthaṅkāras*, were also known by the name of *kevalins*. But these are not the only points of contact between Yoga and Jainism; there are also striking parallels in the ethical sphere which it would be worth while to pursue in a separate study.[4]

What kind of yogic experience does *kaivalya* denote? J. Gonda (1960, I, 312) offered this explanation: 'The various members of Yoga which are as it were arranged in stages have but one purpose, the isolation of the spirit (*Kaivalya*), that is, the union with God. Kaivalya is the experience of the perfect simplicity and uniformity of the nucleus of the personality. This experience [. . .] is one of transcendental bliss infinitely superior to the ordinary state of consciousness, and in it the true being of the yogin expands immensely. The condition of enlightenment is indescribable: one has transcended nature and no longer stands in need of anything and experiences the unity of all existence.' This description of the goal of Yoga is not only fragmentary but also misleading. Apart from the fact that the 'members' of the yogic path cannot be regarded as rungs on a ladder, in what sense can one possibly speak of a union with god? Does *kaivalya* really contain an element of bliss? What does it mean: 'the true being of the *yogin* expands immensely'?

To what degree these strictures are valid is borne out by the actual meaning of *kaivalya* as it emerges from an unprejudiced study of its context in the *Yoga-Sūtra*. Here we find that in II.25 *kaivalya* is used to qualify the word *dṛśi* or 'seeing', which is identical with the 'sheer seeing' (*dṛśi-mātra*) of II.20. If any predication can be made at all of the Self it is this, that the *puruṣa* is of the nature of pure unmitigated Awareness, or, as Patañjali (IV.34) has it, *citi-śakti* or 'power of Awareness'.

Visual experience supplies the most illuminating metaphors to describe this transcendental Awareness, though in earlier days the other sensory and mental experiences also served the same purpose. In a famous passage in the *Bṛhadāranyaka-Upaniṣad* (III.7.22), for instance, Yājñavalkya instructs his disciple thus: '[The Self] is the unseen Seer, the unheard Hearer, the unthought Thinker, the unknown Knower – other than He there is no seer, other than He there is no hearer, other than He there is no thinker, other than He there is no knower. He is the Self, the Inner Controller, the Immortal.'[5]

The expression 'aloneness of seeing' (*dṛśeḥ kaivalyam*, II.25) is not repeated elsewhere in the *Yoga-Sūtra*, but it can be taken to be implied in all other instances where the term *kaivalya* is mentioned. *Kaivalya* is primarily the 'aloneness [of seeing (of the Self)]' and only secondarily, and by implication, aloneness in the sense of emancipation. This strange usage can be explained by those aphorisms which speak of the seeming involvement of the Self with the processes of *prakṛti* or, more precisely, with the states of the psycho-somatic organism. *Kaivalya* is thus the exact antithesis of *saṃyoga* or 'correlation', which refers to the Self's function as the 'seer' of the contents of consciousness.

This is the condition described in aphorism I.4 as *vṛtti-sārūpya* or 'conformity with the fluctuations [of consciousness]'. In contrast to this, *kaivalya* denotes the 'own-form' (*sva-rūpa*) of the 'seer' (*draṣṭṛ*). It supervenes when *saṃyoga*, the correlation between the Self and the contents of consciousness, is disrupted.

Saṃyoga is defined in II.23 as the 'cause of the apprehension of the own-form of the power of the "owner" [and that of] the "owned"' (*sva-svāmi-śaktyoḥ sva-rūpa-upalabdhi-hetuḥ*). In II.24 *avidyā* or 'nescience' is stated as the cause of the correlation. This 'pre-established harmony' (*yogyatā*)[6] between Self (*puruṣa*) and consciousness (*citta*) is of a purely noetic nature. No real substantial intermixing takes place, since an unbridged hiatus is postulated between the Self and *prakṛti*. However, because of the intrinsic immutability (*apariṇāmitva*) of the Self as the principle of Awareness, it is possible for the *puruṣa* to apperceive continuously the on-going transformations of *prakṛti* as mirrored or expressed in a particular consciousness (see IV.18) of a specific organism. This doctrine has its epic antecedents, for instance in XII.210.10): 'The seer, transcending the primary-constituents, [apperceives] the modifications of Nature' (*prakṛteś-ca vikārāṇāṃ draṣṭāram-aguṇa-anvitam*).

As is emphasised in III.35 *puruṣa* and *sattva* (= *citta*) are always 'unmixed' (*asaṃkīrṇa*), and yet somehow the ordinary unenlightened mind fails to perceive this fundamental ontic distinction and literally confuses both principles. The Self is always and irrevocably pure Awareness, whether the mind is operative or idle. Consciousness-of (*citta*) is in perpetual motion and can diminish to the point where one speaks of the inception of unconsciousness, but *citi-śakti* is in no way altered or reduced when a person is hypnotised, asleep or plain unconscious. The Self is quite unaffected by the behaviour of the mind.

This axiom, undoubtedly derived from yogic noumenous experiencing and therefore also only experientially verifiable, has caused some Western critics considerable embarrassment, accustomed as they are to regard consciousness as an attribute of the mental life. In a recent study on the nature of consciousness as viewed from different philosophical angles, P. Bowes (1971, 170-1) made the following pertinent observation: 'One of the reasons why people are inclined to feel that consciousness is a function of the brain is that they identify the conscious with the mental, and the mental, as recent researches in neurophysiology and computer functioning show, can be identified with the physical with some gain in clarity and understanding. If the mental is the physical the conscious must be physical too, for consciousness is an attribute that sometimes qualifies the mental. But the conclusion that the conscious is the physical does not follow if the conscious is something distinct from the mental. This is where Sāṃkhya philosophy comes in, which may have a contribution to make, not in the details of its explanation, much of which is pretty archaic, but in its contention that the conscious is not the mental when the mental is characterised by intelligence, and that the mental has to be explained in terms of the material.'

The notion of the Self as pure underived Awareness is only one side of the doctrine of emancipation; the other is the postulate that man's true identity lies outside the personality complex in the Self. It is this second point which provides the ethical imperative of Yoga which challenges man to dissociate himself from the impermanent states of the body-mind configuration in order to regain true Self-identity. Man's essence is thus the pure Awareness itself. Hence the empirical self must in a certain sense be a mirage. Criticising this interpretation of reality as advocated in Yoga and Sāṃkhya, P. Bowes (1971, 184) contended that Sāṃkhya may be misled by the term 'pure' frequently prefixed to 'transcendental awareness' in order to demarcate it from the empirical consciousness-of (*citta*) which is always a knowing of this or that.[7] She pointed out: 'But the term "pure" has also a moral connotation which suggests that whatever is pure is far more desirable than what is not pure. So consciousness as such, pure consciousness, becomes something with which men ought to identify themselves rather than with empirical consciousness which is relative to its content and hence not pure.'

The concept of freedom as conceived in Yoga is manifestly quite distinct from the western interpretations of it. In a sense man is, essentially, always free because the Self is never entering the mechanisms of *prakṛti*. *Ergo* emancipation is not something which could, strictly speaking, be attained or effected. But in another, empirical sense there is a movement towards the Self *via* purification and noetic catharsis. Emancipation is total transcendence, which amounts to the same as saying that when the essence of man is 'somehow' recovered, man ceases to be man as we know him.

The self-same transcendental Awareness 'shines forth' unalloyed and unabated. Its 'light' is 'mirrored' in those organisms of *prakṛti* which have evolved a sufficient degree of complexity, such as the human organism.[8] It is at this point in time that there arises the vexed problem of identity: the Self-reflective stage of the mind. Thus consciousness-of is in a way a function of pure Awareness and *prakṛti* combined. By manipulating the organismic situation in the form of voluntaristic alterations of consciousness, the mind can gradually be approximated to the pure Awareness. This process is couched in terms of purification (*śuddhi*:[9] the *yogin* must endeavour to remove the 'veils' (*āvaraṇa*) which prevent the transcendental Awareness from manifesting itself in the organism; he must burn up the 'defilements' (*doṣa*) which stain the mirror of his mind and obscure the Self's radiance.

This is basically, though not exclusively, a cognitive cleansing process, as is brought home by such key terms as *viveka-khyāti* (vision of discernment) or *anyatā-khyāti* (vision of distinction). This inner rearrangement or mental purification consists in the main of a gradual but persistent effort at dispelling the various empirical mal-identifications. In other words, the *yogin* assumes *a priori* that the Self is the locus of his true identity and then proceeds to disentangle his multiple misconceptions about his own nature by retracting from everything that exposes itself to him as non-self. And 'non-Self' (*an-ātman*) is absolutely everything that proves to be unstable, finite and sorrowful. Thus severing all contacts with *prakṛtic* identities, the empirical consciousness ultimately collapses for lack of an objective prop. What remains is the pure Awareness itself.

Kaivalya ensues upon the disappearance of even the last trace of defilement (*doṣa*), at which point the *sattva* is, figuratively speaking, as pure as the Self (see III.55). This at least is the definition of *kaivalya* according to the *aṣṭa-aṅga-yoga* tradition quoted (?) by Patañjali. Here *sattva* does not signify one of the three primary-constituents (*guṇa*), but it stands for a condition of the mind which is connected with the 'upward progress of return to the original state'.[10] It can be said to correspond with *liṅga-mātra* in the structural schema of ontogenesis.

It is clear from what has been said hitherto that *kaivalya*, or rather the 'aloneness of seeing', transcends every known state of mind. Strictly speaking, it represents an unknowable. Hence to describe it as an 'experience', as did *inter alia* J. Gonda (1960, I), or worse still as an 'experience of joy', must be recognised as a serious distortion of the true position of Classical Yoga. Likewise, spatial metaphors are out of place, since the Self is an aspatial/atemporal reality. No 'expansion' of anything or into anything can occur.

Equally unsound is the popular idea that *kaivalya* implies a union with the divine. Whatever the reality may be that *kaivalya* stands for – and I do not wish to discard out of hand the idea of a transcendental unity of numinous experiencing – the system of explanation proposed by Patañjali certainly does not leave a niche for such an assumption. Union presupposes a situation of bridgeable separation; yet *īśvara* and *puruṣa* are absolutely and irreversibly co-essential, wherefore the question of a re-linking does not even arise.

In this respect Classical Yoga differs markedly from the teaching of the *Bhagavad-Gītā*, where emancipation is conceived of as a kind of living in the eternal presence of God in a medium of mutual transcendental love-participation (*bhakti*). This is the concept of *brahma-nirvāṇa* as subsisting in the being of God.[11]

Lastly, having cast doubt on the oft-repeated assertion that Patañjali affirmed the plurality of Selves, *kaivalya* can also hardly be said to represent a state in which each Self-monad is reinstated in utmost isolation from the world and from all other Self-monads, as was claimed, among others, by M. Eliade (1973[3], 32). Strictly speaking, *kaivalya* is not anything separate from the Self. Nor is it, properly speaking, a condition or quality of the Self.[12] Nor is it a goal for the Self. It is simply an empirical construct invented to mark off the Self as postulated in the mesh of psycho-somatic existence from the Self as 'verified' after the pseudo-event of liberation.

I am not sure that H. Zimmer (1953[2]) was right in emphasising that *kaivalya* denotes both 'isolation' and 'perfection'. Primarily *kaivalya* appears to be used in a more restricted sense, as describing the Self's uncontaminated purity. This seems to be confirmed by the use of *apavarga* or 'liberation' in II.18, which is regarded as the antithesis of *bhoga* or 'world-enjoyment'. *Apavarga* describes the ethical goal of the *yogin*, the movement towards the Self, and it is to this notion to which H. Zimmer's transcription of the yogic target as 'integration' applies. *Kaivalya*, on the other hand, in so far as it stands for the Self's perfectly autonomous existence, is to be correlated with the condition of apparent linkage (*saṃyoga*) between Self-Awareness and the finite consciousness. *Kaivalya* is the condition of the Self in its transcendental purity as 'the alone' (*kevala*).

V

Psychological Concepts

In response to its soteriological purposes Yoga has developed a peculiar psychology whose primary objective is to assist the *yogin* in reconstituting his consciousness so as to allow the transcendental Self-Awareness to become manifest to the mental apparatus. It is thus an eminently practical endeavour which cannot be separated from the overall philosophical concerns of Yoga and its ethical goals. As a matter of fact there is not even a synonym for what is here called 'psychology'. This significant fact has been fully appreciated by M. Eliade (1973^3, 38), who placed the word in quotation marks.

It must be remembered that any compartmentalisation of the homogeneous structure of Yoga theory into such divisions as 'psychology', 'philosophy' or 'ethics' is no more than an artificial means of promoting the analysis and understanding of a rather differently organised body of knowledge. Because of the prominent practical orientation of the 'psychological' aspect of Yoga, it has occasionally been compared to western psychoanalytical theories and procedures, but the comparison is only conditionally valid.[1]

The fact is that the psychological dimension of Yoga is still a fairly untravelled territory awaiting a far-sighted explorer. There exist a few tentative studies of various aspects of Yoga psychology, mostly by Indian authors, but these do not amount to a great deal and conceptually often leave much to be desired.[2] One of the principal reasons which invalidate, or at least render questionable, many of these well-meaning contributions is a certain semantic naïveté. More often than not their interpretations take little notice of the particular context in which concepts occur. Yet only a scrupulous analysis of the contextual meaning of a concept creates an adequate base for a comparative study and assessment. On the following pages, then, an attempt is made to determine the semantic content of a select number of psychological concepts as they occur in the *Yoga-Sūtra*.

1 *Citta*

The single most important psychological concept employed in Classical Yoga is *citta*. A variety of translations have been suggested for this word, such as 'mind' (R. Prasāda, S. Dasgupta), 'mind-stuff' (J. H. Woods, H. Zimmer), 'internal organ' (G. Jha), 'innere Welt' (J. W. Hauer), 'mind-complex' (G. M. Koelman), 'consciousness' (M. Eliade), 'thinking principle' (M. N. Dvivedī) and 'psychic nature' (C. H. Johnston).

The word *citta* is the perfect passive participle of the verbal root √*cit*, meaning 'to recognise' observe, perceive' and also 'to be bright, to shine'. It is applied wherever psycho-mental phenomena connected with conscious activity are to be expressed. *Citta* is used already in the *Ṛgveda* and the *Atharvaveda* besides the more frequently employed terms *asu* ('life' or 'vital force') and *manas* ('mind').[3] It also appears occasionally in the Upaniṣads.[4] However, it was in constant use by the time of the composition of the *Mahābhārata*, and from then on belonged to the standard psychological vocabulary.

Unlike *manas*, which is used by most other orthodox hindu schools of thought to denote the concept 'mind', the term *citta* appears to be more specifically at home in Yoga. In Sāṃkhya the synonym 'inner organ' (*antaḥkaraṇa*) is found, which is taken to be constituted of *buddhi*, *ahaṃkara* and *manas*.[5] The Yoga commentators, on the other hand, employ the terms *buddhi*, *antaḥkaraṇa* and *citta* rather indiscriminately.

Notwithstanding the fact that Patañjali does not provide a definition of this concept, it is clear from its twenty-two applications in the *Yoga-Sūtra* itself and from the commentaries that *citta* generally denotes the entire mental machinery. It is an umbrella term comprising all the various functionings of the mind. As G. M. Koelman (1970, 100) trenchantly put it, *citta* 'is surely not a separate prakṛitic evolute' in as much as it is not distinct from its component factors, *i.e. buddhi*, etc., whose emergence from the ground of *prakṛti* is the theme of the ontogenetic schema outlined above.

This evinces yet again the holistic approach of Classical Yoga which lays great stress on the organicity of the processes of consciousness and is only secondarily interested in an analytical categorisation of the inner states. Often *citta* conveys simply 'consciousness'. It is impossible to find a single label for it in English. 'Mind-complex' and 'consciousness' should both be borne in mind.

In any event, I believe S. Radhakrishnan (1951[6], II, 345) to be entirely wrong when conjecturing that *citta* is a synonym of the Sāṃkhya *mahat*. Nor do I understand his statement that it 'is the first product of prakṛti, though it is taken in a comprehensive sense, so as to include intellect, self-consciousness and mind' (*ibid.*). Nowhere in the *Yoga-Sūtra* is *citta* regarded as the first evolute of the world-ground, and if it were thus considered, how could it possibly be said to entail the other categories listed by S. Radhakrishnan?

P. Tuxen (1911, 99) and E. Frauwallner (1953, I, 411) are probably mistaken in regarding *manas* as wholly equivalent to *citta*.[6] In one sense *citta* is a comprehensive operational concept which embraces the function of the *sensorium commune* or *manas*, and on the other hand it is 'consciousness' as a non-structural concept. The term *manas* occurs thrice in Patañjali's work, *viz.* I.35; II.53 and III.48. The first and second instances bear out the traditionally intimate association of *manas* with the sensory capacities which are to be checked by withdrawal (*pratyāhāra*) and concentration (*dhāraṇā*). Aphorism III.48, again, speaks of the fleetness (*javitva*) of the *manas* which, if one looks more closely, is said to be consequent on the 'mastery of the senses' (*indriya-jaya*) mentioned in the preceding *sūtra*. This consistent conjunction of *manas* and the senses is far from accidental and reflects pre-classical usage. But this also means that Patañjali most definitely did not treat *manas* and *citta* as synonyms.

Precisely what *citta* entails can be pieced together from the relevant statements in the fourth *pāda*, which deals in a more concentrated way with the philosophical issues of Patañjali's teaching. The following points emerge from an analysis of these references:

(1) *Citta* is in a way the product of both the transcendental Self-Awareness (*puruṣa*) and the insentient world-mechanism (*prakṛti*), for it is said to be 'coloured' or 'affected' (*uparakta*) by the perceived objects as well as by the Self (see IV.23). However, it is not an actual derivative of either. It can thus be characterised as a function of the relation between *puruṣa* and *prakṛti*. For this reason the translation by 'mind-stuff' must be rejected.

(2) In IV.4 *citta* is said to arise from *asmitā-mātra*, which S. Dasgupta (1924, 50) not inappropriately rendered as 'ego-universal'. It is important to understand that no causal dependence is implied here. *Citta* is not a separate *tattva* which could be traced back to *asmitā-mātra* along a direct evolutionary line. *Citta* denotes the whole set of psycho-mental factors as the true evolutes of *asmitā-mātra*. Only

in as much as *citta* is constituted by these individual *tattvas* of the psychic branch of ontogenesis can it be said to have originated from *asmitā-mātra*, which is the point of bifurcation into physical-objective and psychic-subjective categories (*tattva*). In this sense alone can *citta* be regarded as a particularisation or nucleation of *asmitā-mātra*.

(3) Although *citta* is held to be born of the 'single mind' (*eka-citta*) which is none other than *asmitā-mātra*, there are nevertheless many distinct *cittas* which are all real (see IV.16) and not merely attributes of external objects (see IV.15). Nor are they simply products of the imagination of the single mind.

(4) *Citta* is suffused with, and in a certain way structured by, countless 'subliminal-activators' (*saṃskāra*) which form into 'traits' (*vāsanā*) (see IV.24), and it is they that feed the fluctuations (*vṛtti*), thus causing the centrifugality of the mind which actively prevents Self-actualisation.

(5) However, despite the innumerable subliminal traits which are without beginning (see IV.10) and composed of the *saṃskāras* stored in the depth-memory (*smṛti*) (see IV.9), *citta* nonetheless serves the purpose of emancipation (see IV.24). This teleology of *citta* is explained by the 'collaborate activity' (*saṃhatya-kāritva*) of the Self, which consists in the Self's uninterrupted apperception of the ongoings of the mind (see IV.18).

(6) When the Self shines forth in perfect purity, the primary-constituents (*guṇa*) involute, and, with the dissolution of the organism, the mental complex is likewise annihilated (see IV.34). This dissipation of the mental complex upon emancipation is inferred from the fact that the *guṇas* are said to stream back into the transcendental core of Nature.

As is clear from the above, Patañjali operates with a remarkably sophisticated concept of mind which bears a close semblance to certain modern psychological theories. According to him, mind represents a system of dynamic relations which have as their mainstay the complex neurophysiological (= objective-prakṛtic) organism. There are various sub-systems – the evolutionary *tattvas* proper – such as *manas*, which translates the sensory data into concepts, or *asmitā*, which is the focal point of most of the occurring internal processes.

There is also a deep structure, formed by the depth-memory as the storage centre of past mental activity which is not confined to this particular existence but extends backwards *ad infinitum*. Consciousness is energised by this network of *vāsanās* which set up a certain tension, thereby causing the mind to incline towards sensory experience. Externalisation, in turn, leads to the formation of subliminal-activators (*saṃskāra*) which reproduce themselves by means of the fluctuations. The first and foremost task of the yogic process is to intercept this cycle (*saṃskāra* → *vṛtti* → *saṃskāra* . . .) by way of the gradual introversion of consciousness or *pratyak-cetanā*.

In passing it may be pointed out that the question of the spatial extension of the mind which preoccupies especially the later exegetes is something of a pseudo-problem. The mind can be said to have a depth dimension but no location or extension. This is borne out by the ontogenetic model itself. The space-time universe is but the outermost 'rim' of the vast body of *prakṛti* which is essentially aspatial and atemporal but holds the possibility of spatial/temporal existence.

The discussion of the *locus* or the size of the mind was initiated by Vyāsa in his comments on aphorism IV.10. There he reiterates the Sāṃkhya view according to which *citta* contracts or expands in accordance with the bodily dimensions, rather as the light of a lamp spreads out in a spacious palace but becomes confined inside a jar.[7] Yet, he proclaims further, it is only the *vṛtti* ('fluctuation') aspect of consciousness which is subject to such changes in size. Consciousness as such is all-pervasive (*vibhu*) – a doctrine formulated, it seems, to explain the very possibility of omniscience with which the perfected *yogin* is credited.

This important Yoga tenet was rejected by the author of the *Sāṃkhya-Sūtra*, probably a fifteenth-century work. There is no trace of this whole line of enquiry in the *Sāṃkhya-Kārikā* or for that matter in the *Yoga-Sūtra*. Vācaspati Miśra's bisection of consciousness into *kārya-citta* (instrumental consciousness) and *kāraṇa-citta* (causal consciousness) would, I venture to suggest, have left Patañjali unimpressed: firstly, because Vācaspati's interpretation entails an unwarranted hypostatisation of *citta*, and secondly, because an infinite, all-pervasive and hence omniscient *kāraṇa-citta* makes the concept of *puruṣa* (Self) superfluous.

2 *Vṛtti and pariṇāma*

According to Patañjali, the centrifugal consciousness functions in five major ways. These are known as the *vṛttis*. The word stems from the root $\sqrt{vṛt}$ 'to revolve, whirl about' and can mean 'mode of action, conduct, manner of being', etc. G. M. Koelman (1970, 86) equates the term *vṛtti* with *pariṇāma*, but the former expression implies a local activity, whereas the latter connotes serial change in the *Yoga-Sūtra*.

The word *pariṇāma* (from *pari*+ $\sqrt{}$*nām* 'to bend') occurs eleven times in the *Yoga-Sūtra* (*viz.* II.15; III.9, 11, 12, 13, 15, 16; IV.2, 14, 32, 33). To these instances must be added the cognate negative *apariṇāmitva* (IV.18). Although the term does not belong to the oldest stratum of Sanskrit, it is already known to the authors of such pre-Christian texts as the *Śvetāsvatara-Upaniṣad* (V.5)[8] and the *Maitrāyaṇīya-Upaniṣad* (VI.10; III.3). Contrary to E. H. Johnston's (1937, 33) opinion, the word does in fact occur in the *Mahābhārata*, namely in the *Bhagavad-Gītā* (XVIII.37–38) where, however, it is employed in a non-technical sense.[9]

Patañjali in his *Vyākaraṇa-Mahābhāṣya* (I.3.1.11) has the following sentence, which betrays his familiarity with the underlying notion of the word: *jayate'sti vipariṇamate vardhate'pakṣīyate vinaśyati-iti* or 'It is born, changes, grows, wanes and becomes destroyed'. This usage seems to have been known already to Yāska, whose *Nirukta* (I.2) contains a passage which discusses the doctrine of the 'six modifications of becoming' (*ṣaḍ-bhāva-vikārāḥ*) ascribed to a certain Vārṣyāyaṇi. In this connection he supplies this definition: '*vipariṇamata ity-apracyavamānasya tattvād-vikāram* or "Changing" [means] the modification of something-not-divorced ($\sqrt{}$*cyu*) from [its] essence'. Pāṇini, who is later than Yāska, does not seem to make use of this word and its various derivatives.[10]

As was pointed out long ago by W. Liebenthal (1934, 36), whereas the word *vikāra* ('modification') is rare in the Pāli scriptures, its equivalent *vipariṇāma* is fairly frequent; *pariṇāma* in the sense of 'ripening' is also to be met with. Later on the Sautrāntika Buddhists and the adherents of the Vijñānavada availed themselves of this expression. It is also found in the doctrinal sphere of Jainism, as for instance in the *Tattvārthādhigama-Sūtra* (V.41), but is probably of buddhist origin.

According to aphorism I.6 there are five modes of functioning in which the ordinary mind-complex can engage, *viz.* valid cognition (*pramāṇa*), misconception (*viparyaya*), conceptualisation (*vikalpa*), sleep (*nidrā*) and memory (*smṛti*). The word *vṛtti* is applied to any mental content which falls into any of these categories. Used altogether ten times in the *Yoga-Sūtra* (*viz.* I.2, 4, 5, 10, 41; II.11, 15, 50;

III.43; IV.18), *vṛtti* is employed both in a more general sense as 'function, mode of being' (*e.g.* II.15: *guṇa-vṛtti*; II.50 and III.43) and as a *terminus technicus* which refers specifically to such mental activity as falls into the above five behavioural categories of consciousness. In this sense it is often used in the plural (*viz.* I.5; II.11; IV.18).

In the light of this evidence it is incomprehensible that H. Jacobi (1929, 588) should have written, '*vṛtti* is not a philosophical term and hence is not defined by the commentators'. He is doubly wrong here because not only is *vṛtti* definitely a technical designation, it is also defined by Bhoja on at least two occasions. In his *Rāja-Mārtaṇḍa* (I.2) he states: 'The *vṛttis* are forms of modification [of the mind] with a reciprocal relationship between them' (*vṛttayaḥ aṅga-aṅgi-bhāva-pariṇāma-rūpas-tāsām*), and elsewhere (I.5) he says, 'the *vṛttis* are particular modifications of the mind' (*vṛttayaḥ cittasya pariṇāma-viśeṣaḥ*).

The fact that in its technical sense the term refers to specific mental events and not, as is often assumed, to any odd mental content, is clearly borne out by the statement (II.11) that the *vṛttis* are eliminated in meditative absorption (*dhyāna*). This important *sūtra* has always been glossed over. What it says in effect is that no *vṛttis* whatsoever are carried over into *samādhi* but that their complete cessation is a precondition for enstasy to arise. The factors present in *samādhi* are not *vṛttis* but *pratyayas* (*e.g. vitarka*, *vicāra*, etc.).

From this it is also evident that aphorism I.2 does not represent a comprehensive definition of Yoga, and as opposed to M. Sahay (1964), I consider it to be merely a preliminary announcement. M. Sahay's contention that Patañjali meant to prefix *sarva* to the word *vṛtti* is nonsensical. In this particular context *nirodha* is used in a restricted sense, as was fully recognised by the classical exegetes. As will be explained, the process of 'restriction' comprises several levels of application, and the statement of I.2 implies only the lowest degree of restriction (*nirodha*) and not *sarva-nirodha*.

3 *Kleśa, kliṣṭa-akliṣṭa*

The five kinds of *vṛtti* can be either *kliṣṭa* or *akliṣṭa* (see I.5). These terms were respectively translated with 'painful/non-painful' (R. Prasāda, M. N. Dvivedī, G. Jha), 'impure/pure' (M. Eliade), 'afflicted/non-afflicted' (S. Dasgupta), 'hindered/unhindered' (J. H.

Woods) and 'Dränger-behaftet/-nichtbehaftet' (J. W. Hauer). G. M. Koelman (1970), surprisingly enough, does not discuss these twin terms at all, though he refers to the concept of *kleśa*.

Yet this conceptual triad – *kleśa, kliṣṭa* and *akliṣṭa* – constitutes a central aspect of Yoga psychology. All three words are derivatives of the root $\sqrt{}$*kliś* 'to torment, be troubled'. As H. Zimmer (1953[2], 294) aptly remarked, *kliṣṭa* is used 'as an adjective meaning "distressed; suffering pain or misery; faded, wearied, injured, hurt; worn out, in bad condition, marred, impaired, disordered, dimmed, or made faint" [. . .]. A garland, when the flowers are withering, is *kliśta* [*sic*]; and a human being, when the inborn splendour of his nature has been subdued by fatiguing business affairs and cumbersome obligations, is *kliśta* [*sic*].'

In contrast with this general usage of the word in the *Yoga-Sūtra* *kliṣṭa* and its antonym *akliṣṭa* are distinctly technical terms which must be juxtaposed to the concept of *kleśa* or 'cause-of-affliction' denoting, as H. Zimmer (1953[2], 294) put it, 'anything which, adhering to man's nature, restricts or impairs its manifestation of its true essence'. G. M. Koelman (1970, 127) offered a more precise explanation: 'Man is born with certain psychological habits, congenital psychical passions that bind him to cosmic conditions. They blind him, prevent him from discovering what his genuine Self is, make him attached to cosmic life and its allurements, afflict his existence with an endless chain of woes, enmesh him more and more in the net of conditioned existence, and hinder his liberation.'

Patañjali (II.3) distinguishes five types of *kleśa*: nescience (*avidyā*), 'I-am-ness' (*asmitā*), attachment (*rāga*), aversion (*dveṣa*) and the will-to-live (*abhiniveśa*). Each category is carefully defined, and nescience is explained as the nurturing ground of all other types of *kleśa*. This doctrine entails many implications which cannot all be made explicit in this study. For the present purposes it will suffice to make the following observations. The *kleśa* theorem can be said to circumscribe the fact that every organism, on attaining self-consciousness, finds itself in an existential situation where it has become aware of its own awareness but is confused as to the true nature of this awareness, and the organism is, as it were, compelled to act out of a false identity.

This is what is meant by nescience or *avidyā*. It refers to the peculiar cognitive condition of man who fails to recognise that consciousness-of (*citta*) is an epiphenomenon of the transcendental Self-Awareness.

Nonetheless, it would be misleading to ascribe, as did G. J. Larson (1969), to nescience a cosmogonic function which would be more appropriate in the context of Advaita-Vedānta. He stated: 'In the *Yogasūtra* the reason given for the emergence or evolution of the manifest world is *avidyā* ("ignorance"). In this respect there is a fundamental difference between Sāṃkhya and Yoga, for the appearance of the manifest world in classical Sāṃkhya is much more than the result of ignorance. It is the result, rather, of the very nature of *puruṣa* which must become what it is not in order to become what it is' (p. 191).

Apart from G. J. Larson's misapprehension of the precise viewpoint of Patañjali, one may also question his bold speculation that in Sāṃkhya *prakṛti-pariṇāma* is due to the impact of *puruṣa*. This appears to be a later theory which is as yet absent in Īśvara Kṛṣṇa's formulation of Sāṃkhya thought.[11] The recognition of an innate teleology in *prakṛti* does not contradict the simultaneous admission of the autonomous evolution of the *tattvas*.

At any rate, according to Patañjali, *avidyā* is merely a cognitive distortion potent from the very moment self-consciousness emerges. In his own words: 'Nescience is the [false] perception of the permanent in the impermanent, of the pure in the impure, of joyfulness in the sorrowful, of the Self in the non-self' (*anitya-aśuci-duḥkha-anātmasu nitya-śuci-sukha-ātma-khyātir-avidyā*, II.5). Coterminous with this fundamental error is the establishment of a false identity: ' "I-am-ness" is the seeming "one-self-ness" [*i.e.* identity] of the power of seeing [*i.e.* the Self] and that of vision [*i.e.* the mind]' (*dṛg-darśana-śaktyor-eka-ātmatā-iva-asmitā*, II.6).

This mal-identification gives rise to emotive reactions of which Patañjali distinguishes two basic types, *viz.* attachment and aversion. 'Attachment is that which dwells on pleasure' (*sukha-anuśāyī rāgaḥ*, II.7), and 'Aversion is that which dwells on sorrow' (*duḥkha-anuśāyī dveṣaḥ*, II.8). The remaining constituent of this psychological web is the powerful thirst for life, *eros*, the survival instinct about which the *Yoga-Sūtra* affirms: 'The will-to-live, flowing on by its own nature, is rooted even in the sage' (*sva-rasa-vāhī viduṣo'pi tathā rūḍho'bhiniveśaḥ*, II.9).

The *kleśas* provide the dynamic framework of the phenomenal consciousness. They urge the organism to burst into activity, to feel, to think, to want. As the basic emotional and motivational forces they lie at the root of all misery, for Yoga favours the simple equation *anātman* = *duḥkha*, that is to say, as long as man lives out of a false identity in ignorance of his essential nature (which is the Self, *puruṣa*) he remains subject to sorrow and suffering. Hence Vyāsa labels the *kleśas* as 'perversions' (*viparyaya*).[12] Thus the normal human situation can be characterised as the product of a cognitive error, a positive misconstruction of reality, for which there is but one remedy: the recovery of the Self as the true identity of man.

These *kleśas* are thought to have four modes of appearance (see II.4). They may be latent (*prasupta*, lit. 'asleep'), attenuated (*tanu*, lit. 'thin'), temporarily suppressed (*vicchinna*, lit. 'cut off') or fully active (*udāra*, lit. 'coming up'). It is the objective of *kriyā-yoga* to effect their attenuation (*tanūkaraṇa*) which amounts to the cultivation of enstasy (*samādhi-bhāvanā*) (see II.2). No direct attack on the *kleśas* is possible, for every mental activity without exception merely increases the concatenations in the depth-mind.

'Attenuation' is achieved by refusing these forces an outlet in the form of consciousness processes. Their power is partly checked by sensory withdrawal and the accompanying stilling of the mind. In other words, the *yogin* plays the subliminal structures off against each other. By disallowing them to take effect in the conscious mind, he indirectly achieves their mutual annihilation. The underlying process is comparable to that of a millstone which grinds itself away for lack of grain. When even the last subliminal-activator (*saṃskāra*) is exterminated the *kleśas* can be said to be fully destroyed as well.

This intriguing doctrine, 'which is really the foundation of the system of *Yoga* outlined by Patañjali',[13] is epitomised by the two terms *kliṣṭa* and *akliṣṭa*. Vyāsa (I.5) explains *kliṣṭa* as 'caused by the *kleśas*' (*kleśa-hetuka*), but this makes little sense in view of the fact that *akliṣṭa* would consequently have to be understood as 'not caused by the *kleśas*, which is absurd, since all mental activity is *ex hypothesi* engendered by the *kleśas*. Hence Vijñāna Bhikṣu, in his monumental *Yoga-Vārttika* (I.5), proposes a different interpretation of *akliṣṭa*, paraphrasing it 'resulting in *akleśa*' (*akleśa-phalika*).

But what is the nature of this *akleśa*? The answer to this question is supplied in the *Maṇiprabhā* (I.5) by Rāmānanda, where we find the equations *kliṣṭa* = *bandha-phala* (*i.e.* having bondage as its result) and *akliṣṭa* = *mukti-phala* (*i.e.* having liberation as its result). In other words, *akliṣṭa* are those mental events which facilitate the yogic process of the self-destruction of the *kleśas*, whereas *kliṣṭa* describes all other mental activity which merely helps to maintain the potency of the *kleśas*. Thus *akleśa* designates that condition in which the power of the *kleśas* on the mind is partially or completely checked.

4 *Saṃskāra, vāsanā, āśaya*

Hidden behind the overt mental processes lies a vast, inexhaustible pool of stimuli, the so-called 'activators' or *saṃskāras*, which power the machinery of consciousness. These are organised into configurations, known as *vāsanās* or subliminal 'traces' or 'traits', which partly manifest in the idiosyncracies of the individual. This large storehouse of dispositional factors is the dynamic aspect of the deep structure of human personality.

The *saṃskāras* are formed continuously as a result of the individual's world experience. In other words, every thought, feeling and impulse to action must be regarded as an actualisation of the tremendous tension inherent in the subliminal pool. On the other hand, overt mental activity in turn replenishes the subliminal deposit – in this manner perpetuating the vicious circle of phenomenal existence (*saṃsāra*).

The pool of subliminal activators is conceived as pre-individual. This means that although world experience (*bhoga*) somehow reinforces the *saṃskāra* grids, it does not originate them. The newly born individual is by no means a *tabula rasa*. Rather his very birth is the product of the irresistible pull of the subliminal traces. This conception in a way foreshadows the modern notion of the unconscious. However, it is far more simplistic and, furthermore, has been evolved in response to different kinds of questions, having the purpose of explaining certain occurrences during the process of radical introversion and especially during the terminal states of enstasy (*samādhi*).

Unfortunately, Patañjali does not develop this theory in detail but, as with so many other topics, presumes that the reader is acquainted with it. Nonetheless, it is clear from the scanty references in his work that this conception belongs to the core of his system of thought, though of course he cannot be hailed as the genius behind its invention or formulation (see below).

Having sketched the general idea behind this intriguing theory, I will next look more closely at its constituent working parts. To begin with the term *saṃskāra*; this much used Sanskrit word has a wide spectrum of meanings. Composed of the prefix *saṃ-s* and the root $\sqrt{}$*kṛ* 'to do', its most general sense is 'preparation', but in addition it also conveys the idea of 'embellishment, training, ritual action', etc. In yogic contexts, it is habitually translated as 'impression' (J. H. Wood, G. Jha, S. Dasgupta). R. Prasāda (1912) opts for 'habituation', which perhaps would be more appropriate in describing the concept of *vāsanā*.

I prefer to render *saṃskāra* as 'subliminal-activator', thus stressing its dynamic nature. It is far from being a mere imprint, as is suggested by the common translation, 'impression'. This active aspect of the *saṃskāras* is apparent especially from aphorism III.9, where two varieties of *saṃskāra* are distinguished, *viz.* those which lead to the externalisation (*vyutthāna*) of consciousness and those which induce 'restriction' (*nirodha*). Similarly, in I.50 a type of inverted *saṃskāra* is mentioned, which makes its appearance in the highest form of enstasy and which swallos up or rather obstructs all other *saṃskāras*.

Again, the fact that the *saṃskāras* are vestiges of previous mental activity can be inferred from III.18, which states that by means of the immediate apperception (*sākṣātkāra*) of the *saṃskāras* the *yogin* can acquire knowledge of his former embodiments. *Saṃskāra* is thus an active residuum of experience. This concept is beautifully captured in the notion of *bīja* or 'seed' as used in aphorisms I.51 (as *nirbīja*) and III.50 (as *doṣa-bīja*).[14]

Patañjali's concept of *saṃskāra* is ostensibly a mirror-image of the ancient buddhist notion of *saṅkhāra* (Pāli), signifying the conative factors in the nexus of 'conditioned origination' (Pāli: *paṭicca-samuppāda*) or, more precisely, its second link (*nidāna*). In a way the five *kleśas* of Classical Yoga are comparable to the twelvefold *nidāna* nexus or at any rate are equivalent to part of this schema. However, no direct borrowing from Buddhism need be involved here. Speculations about nescience (*avidyā*), sorrow (*duḥkha*) and rebirth (*punar-janman*) are pan-Indian property.

The next term to be considered is *vāsanā*. Although often used by the exegetes and modern interpreters as a synonym of *saṃskāra*, *vāsanā* really stands for a different concept. *Vāsanā*, which is a derivative of the root $\sqrt{vas}$ 'to dwell, abide, remain', is mentioned only twice in the *Yoga-Sūtra* (*viz.* IV.8, 24) and in both instances in the plural. It has variously been translated as 'subconscious impression' (J. H. Woods), 'impression' (G. Jha) and 'residual potency' (R. Prasāda). J. W. Hauer (1958) rendered it as 'Einwohnung' and correctly delineated it in his translation from the concept of *saṃskāra*; however, in a footnote (p. 469, fn. 7) he contradicted himself again with the unwise remark that *vāsanā, saṃskāra* and *karma-āśaya* can be regarded as synonyms. He failed to appreciate that Patañjali would hardly have introduced three different terms to express one and the same idea, particularly an idea of such central importance.

According to aphorism IV.8, the origination of the *vāsanās* is to be linked up with the fruition (*vipāka*) of man's activity. Whilst the activity of the adept *yogin* is thought to be (see IV.7) neither 'white' nor 'black', that of the ordinary mortal is threefold. This somewhat recondite aphorism is explained by the doctrine of moral retribution as it has been current in India ever since the early Upaniṣads, where it was first announced.

What Patañjali appears to be saying is this. Ordinarily every action's fruition can be classified as either 'black' (*kṛṣṇa*), *i.e.* 'non-meritorious' (*apuṇya*, see I.33; II.14), or 'white' (*śukla*), *i.e.* 'meritorious' (*puṇya*), or, I presume, as mixed.[15] In contradistinction the *yogin* – his mental complex being fully inclined towards total dissolution (*pratiprasava*) – does not generate any action which could be thus typified. By *vipāka* or fructification is meant not the 'outcome' of an act on the empirical plane, but its 'moral consequence', which is expressed in terms of the production of corresponding *vāsanā* configurations. These *vāsanās*, in their turn, act as the propelling force for the creation of a new individual organism after the death of the present subject. They must be considered as aspatial/atemporal constellations 'located' in the deep structure of the microcosm.

The question of how these subliminal configurations can bridge the gap between two existences is explained in a rather difficult *sūtra* (IV.9) which reads: *jāti-deśa-kāla-vyavahitānām-apy-ānantaryaṃ smṛti-saṃskārayor eka-rūpatvāt.* J. H. Woods (1966[3]) translated this as follows: 'There is an uninterrupted [causal] relation [of subconscious-impressions], although remote in species and point-of-space and moment-of-time, by reason of the correspondence between memory and subliminal-impressions.'

In accordance with Vyāsa's scholium, J. H. Woods linked *ānantarya* or 'uninterrupted [causal] relation' with the word *saṃskāra*, yet this lacks in clarity. *Ānantarya*, it seems, refers to the causal dependence between the original input into the *vāsanā* pool and the resultant re-translation of the *vāsanā* code into a specific spatio-temporal existence. This homogeneity between cause and effect is guaranteed by the 'uniformity' (*eka-rūpatva*) between the subliminal-activators (*saṃskāra*) and the depth-memory (*smṛti*). Hence I would rephrase the above translation as follows: 'Although [the resultant spatio-temporal existence] is remote [in terms of] type, place and time, [there is nonetheless] a causal-relation [between the original subliminal input and the resultant existence] because of the uniformity between the subliminal-activators and the depth-memory.'

I have rendered the word *smṛti* as 'depth-memory' to indicate that what is meant here is not really the ordinary 'memory', but the *vāsanā* concatenations peculiar to a particular individual. Furthermore, I propose that this is possibly identical with *asmitā-mātra*, which is said to be (see IV.5) the root of the individual mind-complexes or *cittas*. It is quite likely that *smṛti* in I.43 has the very same meaning, since it cannot stand for the ordinary memory (in the sense of 'recollection') – considered to be one of the five categories of *vṛtti* – which is eliminated in the process of meditative absorption (see II.11). The above contention is not as far-fetched as it may seem *prima facie*, if one recalls that Yoga postulates a 'subtle' (*sūkṣma*) counterpart to the overt reality as we know it.

In this connection aphorism IV.10 must be taken into account, which describes the *vāsanās* as 'beginningless' (*anāditva*) in view of the perpetuity of the primal-will (*āśis*). How could the ordinary memory be said to store the entire matrix of *vāsanās* shared by all beings? In passing I wish to draw attention to the word *āśis*, usually translated by 'desire'. Patañjali employs this relatively rare term to express the primordial drive inherent in *prakṛti* which, by means of the *vāsanā* patterns, leads to ever new phenomenalisations. Possibly the concept of *abhiniveśa* (see II.9) is identical with this notion; it can be regarded as a manifestation of *āśis* in the life of a particular entity. This primordial 'survival instinct' can be conceptualised as the counter-tendency to the drive towards 'self-transcendence', equally innate in Nature and without which the yogic aspiration for emancipation (*apavarga*) would remain on the level of wishful thinking and phantasy.

In order to denote the total stock of *saṃskāras* which have been called into existence by the volitional activity in either the present incarnation or in past existences and which are the determinative factors of future embodiments, Patañjali introduces the concept of *āśaya*. The literal meaning of this word, mentioned only in I.24 and II.12, is 'deposit' (from *ā* + √*śī* 'to lie, rest').

G. M. Koelman (1970, 50, fn. 100) translated the compound *karma-āśaya* as 'moral-value-deposit' explaining it as 'the sum-total of merits and demerits'. The idea behind the theory of *karman* or, more accurately, *karma-vipāka* ('fructification of action') is this: no action, or volition, is value neutral. Every action has a value in terms of an objective framework of reference. In other words, the cosmic order is a moral one, and the physical law of causality is extended, *mutatis mutandis*, to the realm of ethical behaviour.

Driven by the *kleśas*, the 'deposit' bears fruit, *viz.* birth, life and world-experience (see II.13). The impact of this subliminal powerhouse can make itself felt not only in the present (*dṛṣṭa* 'seen') existence but also in future (*adṛṣṭa* 'unseen') births (see II.12). The *karma*-residue can, moreover, be acute (*sa-upakrama*) or deferred (*nir-upakrama*) (see III.22), and this can be made the subject of enstatic constraint (*saṃyama*) (see III.18). Depending on the nature of the *vāsanās* or *saṃskāra* chains, which may be due to meritorious or demeritorious volitional activity, the world experience (*bhoga*) is characterised by either delight (*hlāda*) or distress (*paritāpa*) (see II.14).

There is no doubt in Patañjali's mind that even though there may be moments of happiness and even euphoria in life, all joy is deceptive because it is intrinsically transient, and sorrow (*duḥkha*) is woven into the very fabric of phenomenal existence. In his own words (II.15): *pariṇāma-tāpa-saṃskāra-duḥkhair-guṇa-vṛtti-virodhāc-ca duḥkham-eva sarvaṃ vivekinaḥ*, or 'Because of the sorrow in the [continual] transformation [of the world-ground], [in] the anguish [and in] the subliminal-activators and on account of the conflict between the movements of the *guṇas* – to the discerning [*yogin*] all is but sorrow'.

Hence it is sorrow which is to be overcome (see II.16). The means by which *duḥkha* can be surmounted is the disconnection of the correlation (*saṃyoga*) between the 'seer' and the 'seen', that is, the realisation of the innate Self as being apart from all accidental or epiphenomenal events of the mind-complex. This brings us back to the yogic process itself.

5 *Nirodha*

Yoga utilises a great variety of instruments to disrupt the continuum of phenomenal existence, to break the incessant revolution of *prakṛti* which holds no promise of stability or security. At the bottom of all these means lies an identical process, known as *nirodha* or 'restriction'. There is a good deal of misunderstanding about this term, which has already led the classical exegetes astray. It is crucial for a clear comprehension of the yogic path to clarify this important concept. The source of the confusion is the fact that *nirodha* designates both the *process* of restriction and the *state* of restrictedness – a distinction which Vyāsa *et al.* have blatantly ignored.

The word is derived from *ni* + $\sqrt{}$*rudh* 'to restrain' and is mentioned in I.2, 12, 51 and III.9. In contrast to Vyāsa's conjectures, accepted *tout court* by his successors, the important *sūtra* I.2 (*yogaś-citta-vṛtti-nirodhaḥ*) does not use *nirodha* in the sense of 'restrictedness'. Vācaspati Miśra's contention that 'Yoga is that particular state of the mind-complex in which the fluctuations [such as] *pramāṇa* and so forth are restricted'[16] is definitely erroneous. Nor can this aphorism be interpreted as implying that '[the goal of] Yoga is the restrictedness of the fluctuations of consciousness', since the ultimate destination of the *yogin* is not the inhibition of the five modes of mental activity of the externalised consciousness but 'the aloneness of seeing' (*dṛśeḥ kaivalya*). Rather, it must be concluded that aphorism I.2 gives out a preliminary definition of Yoga as the process of restriction, commencing with the inhibition of the *vṛttis*.

This need not necessarily conflict with *sūtra* I.3, where the initial word *tadā* ('then') does not have to imply 'immediately upon the restriction of the *vṛttis*'. Also, the phrase *draṣṭuḥ sva-rūpe'vasthanam* may not refer to *kaivalya* at all but simply to the Self as it *appears* in relative purity in *samādhi*: the stillness of the mind-complex permits a centralised experiencing in which, although the level of the transcendental Self has not yet been reached, the *puruṣa*'s presence is keenly felt as the stable centre within the enstatic process.

As is borne out by a candid examination of the relevant statements of the *Yoga-Sūtra*, the process of restriction is not confined to the pentad of fluctuations but is a multi-level happening which coincides with the yogic process of unification *per se*. This, incidentally, sheds new light also on the concept of *abhyāsa* or 'practice'. In point of fact, restriction comprises three distinct levels of application:

(1) restriction of the fluctuations (*vṛtti-nirodha*),
(2) restriction of the presented-ideas (*pratyaya-nirodha*),
(3) restriction of the subliminal-activators (*saṃskāra-nirodha*).

Nirodha sets in as soon as the *yogin* withdraws his senses from the external world by means of the technique of *pratyāhāra* conducive to one-pointed concentration. In III.9 it is stated that, with the disappearance of the 'subliminal-activators of emergence' (*vyutthāna-saṃskāra*), the 'subliminal-activators of restriction' (*nirodha-saṃskāra*) emerge. This means that during the normal waking (centrifugal) condition of consciousness those subliminal-activators are effective which lead to wakefulness (*vyutthāna*), whilst the withdrawal of the senses involves such subliminal-activators as will countercheck the externalising tendency of the mind. *Vṛtti-nirodha* can mean either the partial or the complete (*sarva*) restriction of the five types of mental fluctuation, thus covering every phase of sense-withdrawal, concentration and meditative absorption. It is an on-going process with increasing restrictedness.

Valid cognition (*pramāṇa*) and faulty cognition (*viparyaya*), both of which are dependent on an objective substratum, are the first to be eliminated in the internalisation procedure. There is no more contact with the external environment once meditative absorption (*dhyāna*) is established. *Vikalpa* or 'predicate-relation', as J. H. Woods (1966[3]) translated this term, is also soon restricted. Far more difficult is the elimination of sleep (*nidrā*). It is a common experience that during the first attempts at meditative absorption, the mind instead of reaching the restricted (*niruddha*) state often lapses into sleep. The untrained mind is unable to sustain the intense concentration required for more than brief spells only and quickly succumbs to exhaustion.

However, the greatest hindrance of all is the powerful human memory which constantly populates the consciousness space with thoughts, images and moods. Its complete control can only be achieved after extensive practice of *dhyāna*. 'Memory' (*smṛti*) refers here to the actual process of remembering and not, as in I.43, to the depth-memory, though both are of course intimately related. In passing it may be pointed out that Patañjali's enumeration of the *vṛttis* is far from arbitrary. His arrangement is according to the *vṛttis'* relation with the external environment, *pramāṇa* being as it were the outermost and *smṛti* the innermost of the diverse mental activities.

Since the stoppage of the fluctuations is clearly stated to be effected in *dhyāna* (see II.11), *nirodha* cannot possibly be identified with enstasy (*samādhi*); the classical commentators are definitely at fault on this crucial point.[17] The essential happening in the enstatic states of consciousness can be described as the gradual restriction of the 'presented-ideas' (*pratyaya*). As will be shown, these must not be confused with the *vṛttis*.

On a still deeper level of restriction, the very propensity to form *pratyayas* and *vṛttis* is brought under control. This is *saṃskāra-nirodha*, which, when completed successfully, is known as *sarva-nirodha* or total restrictedness and is commensurate with the final breakthrough to the Self's aloneness (*kaivalya*). I will discuss this phase in conjunction with *samādhi*.

6 *Pratyaya*

The word *pratyaya* (from *prati* + $\sqrt{i}$ 'to go') occurs no fewer than ten times in the *Yoga-Sūtra* (*viz.* I.10, 18, 19; II.20; III.2, 12, 17, 19, 35 and IV.27), and it is an important technical expression. This fact has not been recognised by the Sanskrit exegetes, who occasionally employ *pratyaya* in the sense of 'cause' and then again as descriptive of some mental content. Neither the *Yoga-Bhāṣya* nor the *Tattva-Vaiśāradī* provides a definition of this term in its second meaning of 'idea, notion'.

When we turn to Bhoja, slightly more information about the meaning of this concept can be obtained. He describes, in his *Rāja-Mārtaṇḍa*, *pratyaya* as 'knowledge' (*jñāna*) (see III.2) and elsewhere (II.20) speaks of these presented-ideas as 'knowledges tinctured by an object' (*viṣaya-uparaktāṇi jñānāni*). He thus understands it as a kind of awareness of something.

This appears to be the meaning of the term throughout the *Yoga-Sūtra*. Even aphorism I.19 can be adequately interpreted in this way (see below). I consider this expression as belonging to the core technical vocabulary of Classical Yoga, together with such *termini* as *vṛtti*, *citta* or *nirodha*, etc.

In the commentaries *pratyaya* and *vṛtti* are frequently used synonymously, but this usage is incorrect if it is intended to reflect Patañjali's viewpoint. For the presence of a *pratyaya* does not necessarily imply the simultaneous occurrence of a *vṛtti*. This is evident from the fact that there appear in *samādhi* various types of awareness units, e.g. *vitarka*, *vicāra*, etc., which cannot be designated as *vṛtti* but which pertain to the *pratyaya* category.

It appears that the term *pratyaya* is specifically applied to the phenomenon of awareness as it presents itself in a consciousness that rests on an object of some kind. The analogue of *vṛtti* in the enstatic consciousness is not *pratyaya* but *prajñā* or gnostic knowing in which the object is apprehended directly and from within itself, as it were. On the basis of these considerations I suggest the following taxonomy:

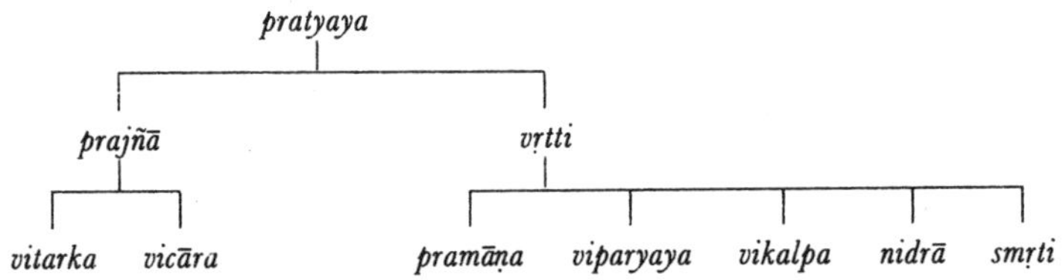

The term *prajñā*, standing for the cognitive elements present in enstasy (*samādhi*), is inferred from its usage in such aphorisms as II.27, which speaks of a 'sevenfold gnosis' (*saptadhā prajñā*), and III.5, which has the phrase 'the flashing-forth of transcendental-insight' (*prajñā-āloka*), and, above all, from the term *saṃprajñāta*, describing all modalities of enstasy which have an objective 'prop' (*ālambana*).

However, there is one single exception to this rule: in I.49 *prajñā* has the meaning of 'knowledge' usually designated by the word *jñāna*. This deviation can be explained by the context, from which it is apparent that the author, for the sake of convenience, retained the word *prajñā* as used in the immediately preceding *sūtra*. Perhaps even a pun is intended which a modern writer would have expressed by placing the term *prajñā* in inverted commas: 'The scope [of this gnostic insight] is distinct from the "insight" [gained from] tradition and inference owing to [its] particular purposiveness' (*śruta anumāna-prajñābhyām-anya-viṣayā viśeṣa-arthatvāt*).[18]

A. Janáček (1957) attempted to show that *pratyaya* corresponds with the Pavlovian concept of 'impulse', but J. W. Hauer (1958, 464, fn. 6) cast serious doubt on this interpretation, though he conceded that in the fourth book of Patañjali's work (which he regarded as a later appendix) the term *pratyaya* may possibly have the meaning suggested by A. Janáček. Concerning the first three *pādas*, J. W. Hauer's translation wavers between 'awareness' and 'cause' as fit renderings of *pratyaya*. However, it is quite unnecessary to assume this double connotation, as all the relevant *sūtras* can satisfactorily be understood when one gives *pratyaya* the uniform meaning of a specific noetic factor.

Unlike *prajñā* and *vṛtti*, which are classified by their functional characteristics, *pratyaya* is more a relational concept in which the content of consciousness is defined in its relation to the transcendental Self as the permanent apperceiver of all ideation. Hence the most congenial translation of this term is the one proposed by J. H. Woods

(1966³), namely 'presented-idea'. This was accepted, *inter alia*, by G. M. Koelman (1970), one of the few scholars to make a consistent attempt at developing a critical vocabulary for expressing yogic concepts in English. Still, he failed to recognise the leading significance of this concept in the psychology of Classical Yoga and consequently did not realise that *pratyaya* must be given the constant value of 'presented-idea' in the *Yoga-Sūtra*.

To quote but one instance, what does G. M. Koelman (1970, 185) mean when translating aphorism I.10 as 'Sleep is a fluctuation supported by the coming to the fore of the absence [of the waking and dreaming states]'?[19] It seems to me that the compound *abhāva-pratyaya* is far more intelligibly rendered as 'the presented-idea of the non-occurrence [of conscious contents]'. Since *nidrā* is a *vṛtti* it must be based on a *pratyaya* of some kind; hence *abhāva-pratyaya* cannot really mean 'the absence of *pratyayas*'.[20]

This was fully recognised by K. Bhattacharyya (1956, I, 256), who wrote, 'Presentation of a content that is known as real is pramāṇa, of a content that is known as unreal is viparyaya and of a content that appears real even when it is known as unreal is vikalpa; while presentation of a content *as* presented – i.e. presentation of presentation is smṛti and presentation of the absence of presentation is nidrā.' In this way sleep is adequately demarcated from the condition of restriction (*nirodha*) in which all fluctuations are restricted. This is in conformity with Vyāsa's exposition of sleep. He seeks to demonstrate that there is mental activity of some kind even in deep sleep, by pointing out that when a person awakes he usually 'recollects' that he has slept either well or badly.

Likewise, the phrase *bhava-pratyaya* in I.19 need not be taken to signify 'caused by wordly [means]' as is the contention of the exegetes (see also J. H. Woods, 1966³). Rather, it must be explained in conjunction with I.18. These two aphorisms read as follows: *virāma-pratyaya-abhyāsa-pūrvaḥ saṃskāra-śeṣo'nyaḥ – bhava-pratyayo videha-prakṛti-layānām.* Aphorism I.18 undoubtedly defines the ultra-cognitive enstasy (*asaṃprajñāta-samādhi*), and *virāma-pratyaya* must be translated as 'presented-idea of cessation' and is not to be confused with *abhāva-pratyaya*. The 'previous practice' (*abhyāsa-pūrva*) refers to the cognitive enstasy (*saṃprajñāta-samādhi*) in which the restriction of the presented-ideas (*pratyaya-nirodha*) is gradually effected. On the other hand, the compound *bhava-pratyaya* obviously signifies 'presented-idea of becoming', which describes the contents of consciousness of those who have failed to transcend the realm of *prakṛti* and have lost sight of the goal of liberation from the fetters of Nature *in toto*.[21]

VI
Practice Concepts

1 *Abhyāsa and vairāgya*

The yogic path as formulated by Patañjali appears as a bi-polar process of gradual internalisation. All techniques are formally subsumed under the two categories of *abhyāsa* and *vairāgya* respectively. The former may be circumscribed as the actualisation of the One and the latter as the elimination of the Many. In L. A. Singh's (1970, I, 108) words, 'In modern terminology, abhyāsa may be conceived as the process of canalisation and re-conditioning; while vairāgya may be seen as a process of de-conditioning. By breaking the associations between motives and goals, of lower levels of psychological development by a process of de-conditioning and then forming new associations between motives and higher goals through a process of re-conditioning one gradually rises from lower to higher levels of affecto-motivational development.'

Abhyāsa and *vairāgya* are thus the two poles of any form of Yoga and, indeed, of any spiritual discipline whatsoever. This point is seldom understood.[1] Vyāsa illustrates the functional interdependence of both poles in a striking simile: *citta-nadī nāma-ubhayato vāhinī vahati kalyāṇāya vahati pāpāya ca, yā tu kaivalya-prāgbhārā viveka-viṣaya-nimnā sā kalyāṇa-vahā, saṃsāra-prāgbhārā'viveka-viṣaya-nimnā pāpa-vahā, tatra vairāgyeṇa viṣaya-srotaḥ khilī-kriyate viveka-darśana-abhyāsena viveka-srota udghāthyata ity-ubhaya-adhīnaś-citta-vṛtti-nirodhaḥ* (I.12): 'The stream of consciousness flows in both [directions]. It flows to the good, and it flows to the bad. The one commencing with discernment (*viveka*) and terminating in *kaivalya* flows to the good. The one commencing with lack-of-discernment (*aviveka*) and terminating in conditioned-existence (*saṃsāra*) flows to the bad. Through dispassion (*vairāgya*) the flowing out to the sense-objects is checked, and through the practice (*abhyāsa*) of the vision of discernment the stream of discernment is laid bare. Thus the restriction of the fluctuations of consciousness is dependent upon both [*abhyāsa* and *vairāgya*].'[2]

This bi-polarity of the yogic path was first brought out in the *Bhagavad-Gītā*, which in fact employs the very same terms used by Patañjali to designate the two poles, and it is as good as certain that he was fully conversant with this old Yoga scripture. The stanza in question is VI.35 which reads: *asaṃśayaṃ mahā-bāho mano durnigrahaṃ calam, abhyāsena tu kaunteya vairāgyeṇa ca gṛhyate*, 'The mind, o strong-armed [Arjuna], is undoubtedly unsteady and difficult to control. Yet through practice and dispassion, o son-of-Kuntī, it can be seized.' This dyadic analysis of the yogic path has survived into the post-classical period of Yoga, as is evident from the encyclopedic *Yoga-Vāsiṣṭha* (II.13.40, V.14.66, etc.); it can even be met with in the *Sāṃkhya-Sūtra* (III.36) and certain Vedānta texts such as Śaṅkara's *Viveka-Cūḍāmaṇi* (374).

Abhyāsa (from *abhi* + $\sqrt{\bar{a}s}$ 'to abide, engage in') does not occur in the earlier strata of hindu literature, where it is replaced by the term *śrama* or 'exertion'.[3] Its first mention is in the *Bhagavad-Gītā* (see VI.35, 44; VIII.8; XII.9, 10, 12; XVIII.36) and the *Śvetāśvatara-Upaniṣad* (I.14), and it is also widely employed in the epic. In its non-philosophical usage the word *abhyāsa* has the meaning of 'repetition, habit', and some of this connotation is carried over into Patañjali's concept of 'practice', as is clear from aphorisms I.13 and I.14: *tatra sthitau yatno'bhyāsaḥ – sa tu dīrgha kāla-nairantarya-satkāra-āsevito dṛḍha-bhūmiḥ*, 'Practice is the [repeated] effort to stabilise [the mind-complex]. However, this [practice] [gains] firm ground [only when it] is cultivated for a long time, uninterruptedly [and with full] attention.'

Nonetheless, S. Dasgupta's (1930, 331) rendering of *abhyāsa* as 'habit' is incorrect, and in fact elsewhere (p. 61) he translated it quite appropriately as 'practice'. To sum up: ' "Practice" stands for the concentrated inner application to the realisation of the transcendental Being which constitutes the essence of all yogic operations. It consists in the careful discrimination between the real and wholesome on the one hand and the transient and all that is unworthy of human motivation on the other. It is the inwardness and unification resulting from this enlightened discernment.'[4]

It may be noted here that in I.32 (*eka-tattva-abhyāsa*),[5] and in I.18 (*virāma-pratyaya-abhyāsa*), the word *abhyāsa* does not appear to be intended in the above formal sense but probably corresponds with the notion of 'exercise' as a specific instance of 'practice'.

Like its positive correlative the negative pole, *vairāgya*, ranks with the post-vedic vocabulary. It does not seem to have been in use prior to the *Bhagavad-Gītā*. Patañjali defines this second constituent of the path as follows: *dṛṣṭa-anuśravika-viṣaya-vitṛṣṇasya vaśīkāra-saṃjñā vairāgyam*, 'Dispassion is the consciousness of mastery of [the *yogin* who is] without thirst for seen and revealed objects'. *Dṛṣṭa* denotes the things visible, that is, the ordinary objects of our pleasure – seeking mind, whereas *anuśravika* (from *anu* + √*śru* 'to hear') applies to objects revealed by the sacred tradition, such as the promised joys of heaven. Dispassion, as understood by Patañjali, is not so much a specific act of non-attachment as a state of mind; it is the 'consciousness of mastery' accruing from the persistent struggle to disengage the mind from everything that is inimical to its internalisation.

Patañjali knows of two degrees of dispassion. He says (I.16): *tat-paraṃ puruṣa-khyāter-guṇa-vaitṛṣṇyam*, 'The superior [form of] this [dispassion] is the non-thirsting for the *guṇas* [which results] from the vision of the Self'. The orbit of the lower degree of *vairāgya* embraces every prakṛtic entity or function except the triple primary forces or *guṇas* into which all manifest and immaterial objects ultimately resolve. But the *yogin* must dissociate himself even from these by realising the higher degree of dispassion which discloses the Self to his enstatic view. This implies the resolution of the entire cognitive apparatus and, in the last analysis, the complete deletion of the individual cosmos.

It may be conjectured that the differentiation into two degrees of consummation as regards dispassion may have its parallel in *abhyāsa*. Tentative evidence for this supposition is found in I.18,[6] where the ultra-cognitive enstasy (*asaṃprajñāta-samādhi*) is covertly referred to as the 'other' (*anya*). It is said to follow upon the 'practice of the cessation of presented-ideas' which is the objective of *saṃprajñāta-samādhi*. Granted that this is tenable, the following correlation is possible:

ordinary *vairāgya* ordinary *abhyāsa*	in combination bring about	*vṛtti-nirodha* ↓ *pratyaya-nirodha*
higher *vairāgya* higher *abhyāsa*	in combination bring about	*saṃskāra-nirodha* ↓ *sarva-nirodha*

2 *Pratyāhāra, dhāraṇā, dhyāna*

The restriction of the five modes of *vṛtti* or mental activity, as the first stage of a protracted process ending in the total abolition of consciousness, is effected by means of the combined practice of sense-withdrawal (*pratyāhāra*), concentration (*dhāraṇā*) and meditative-absorption (*dhyāna*). As these form three phases of a continuum, as it were, I propose to treat them together. Patañjali himself prefers a different arrangement in so far as he brings concentration (*dhāraṇā*), meditative-absorption (*dhyāna*) and enstasy (*samādhi*) under the collective heading of 'inner members' (*antar-aṅga*). Their collective practice is, moreover, denoted by the concept of 'constraint' (*saṃyama*). The reason for his exclusion of *pratyāhāra* would appear to be simply that this is not a purely mental exercise but involves the sensory apparatus.

Pratyāhāra[7] (from *prati* + *ā* + $\sqrt{hṛ}$ 'to hold') is defined in aphorism II.54 as 'the imitation as it were of the own-form of consciousness by the senses disuniting [themselves from] their [respective] objects' (*sva-viṣaya-asaṃprayoge cittasya sva-rūpa-anukāra-iva-indriyāṇāṃ pratyāhāraḥ*). This process has been described in many Yoga texts, and there is little ambiguity about the technique, which can be perfectly understood on the basis of the psychology of attention.

There is a certain degree of sensory inhibition in every kind of mental concentration. As the focus of attention narrows to a strictly confined *locus*, awareness of the surroundings is gradually lost. In Yoga, of course, complete cessation of all sensory activity is aimed at. As the *Bhagavad-Gītā* (II.58) puts it: *yadā saṃharate ca-ayaṃ kūrmo'ṅgāni-iva sarvaśa, indriyāṇi-indriya-arthebhyas-tasya prajñā pratiṣṭhitā*, 'And when he draws in on every side his senses from the objects of the senses as a tortoise [draws in its] limbs – [his] gnosis is well established'. Elsewhere in the great epic of the Bharatas (*e.g.* XII.188.5) the same process is described as 'making into a ball' (*piṇḍi-kṛtya*) or compressing the host of senses (*piṇḍī-kṛtya-indriya-grāmam*). The metaphor of the tortoise is more often used in ontological contexts to illustrate the process of creation and resorption (see *e.g.* *Mahābhārata* XII.239.4; also 239.17 = 239.27).

This non-deployment of the senses is to be understood as the positive effort not to engage in sensory perceptions, as the deliberate attempt to disregard sensory stimuli. Initially arousal is still possible provided that the stimulus is sufficiently strong (*e.g.* a loud noise, a push, etc.), but as the exercise proceeds, control of the afferent functions becomes increasingly more perfect, until total sensory anaesthesia is achieved. This is what is meant by the expression *paramā-vaśyatā* or 'supreme obedience' of the senses (see II.55).

Incidentally, this 'generalised inhibition' is prepared and facilitated by the muscular control effected through the practice of posture of *āsana* and of respiratory stoppage or *prāṇāyāma*. Here, modern neurophysiology confirms the experiential wisdom of Patañjali and his predecessors (see T. R. Kulkarni, 1972, 99 ff.).

G. M. Koelman (1970, 175–6), who singled out four levels of yogic interiorisation, remarked about the practice of *pratyāhāra* that 'it is difficult to situate' in the arrangement proposed by him. 'Though it is in a sense somatic, in as much as physiologically the senses no longer react to external stimuli, and is also ethical in character to the extent that it is aimed at and brought about by the heroic practice of universal detachment, yet we think it is already the threshold of the psychological level. "Withdrawal of the senses" forms the bridge and is the cumulative result of the previous practices, and opens the door to one-pointed concentration.' The four levels distinguished by G. M. Koelman are:

(1) the somatic level, which has as its goal the pacification of the body;
(2) the ethical level, intended for the purification and stabilisation of the mind;
(3) the psychological level, entailing a frontal attack on the empirical mind which is to be transcended;
(4) the metaphysical level, which is identical with emancipation, that is, the transcendental realisation of the Self.

This is a useful model which in a way complements Patañjali's distinction between the 'external members' (*bahir-aṅga*) and 'internal members' (*antar-aṅga*) of the eightfold path (see III.7).

Perseverant practice of sense-withdrawal induces concentration or *dhāraṇā*, characterised by Patañjali as follows: *deśa-bandhaś-cittasya dhāraṇā* (III.1) or 'Concentration is the binding of consciousness to [a single] *locus*'. This technique consists in a focusing of attention, a mental zeroing-in on one topic to the exclusion of all others. It is also referred to in aphorism I.32 as 'the practice of a single principle' (*eka-tattva-abhyāsa*). T. R. Kulkarni (1972, 118) aptly described the underlying process as 'a general "shrinking" of the mind, leaving only a smaller portion of concentrated mental activity'. He also suggested that the concept of the 'neuronal model' of sensory stimulus, as developed by E. N. Sokolov (1963), may possibly be an explanation of this phenomenon in neuro-physiological terms. Nevertheless, it must be stressed here that however instructive these parallels are one must not succumb to the reductionist fallacy of taking them to be sufficient explanations of what is essentially a psychological not a biological, happening.

In I.35 the expression 'holding the mind in steadiness' (*manasaḥ sthiti-nibandhanī*) is found, which invites comparison with the statement of III.1. Whereas the latter is intended as a formal description of an actual technique, the former aphorism evidently speaks of a result of this concentration, namely *nibandhana*, the 'steady' condition of the mind being in this case the concomitant phenomenon of a yogic experience known as *pravṛtti* or extra-ordinary sensory activity.

The centre of attention, or *locus* of concentration, can be any object whatsoever, as long as it is properly 'interiorised'. Preferred *loci* are the bodily centres such as the 'navel wheel' (*nābhi-cakra*, III.29), the 'throat well' (*kaṇṭha-kūpa*, III.30), the 'tortoise duct' (*kūrma-nāḍī*, III.31), the heart (*hṛdaya*, III.34) and the 'light in the head' (*mūrdha-jyotis*, III.32). Patañjali, moreover, lists such non-somatic 'topics' as the sun (*sūrya*, III.26), the moon (*candra*, III.27), the pole-star (*dhruva*, III.28), etc., and purely conceptual items like friendliness (*maitrī*, III.23), strength (*bala*, III.24), etc. In addition there is the recitation (*japa*) of the syllable *oṃ* signifying *īśvara* (see I.27–8), which is an exercise of no mean significance in Classical Yoga.

Anything at all can serve as a 'prop' for concentration, provided it is found fit (see I.39) to narrow consciousness to a spot and to sustain it in this reduced state over a sufficient period of time. An object of some kind seems to be called for in order to avert the ever-present danger of a plain relapse into unconsciousness. The reduction of consciousness to a specific pre-selected point forestalls its premature collapse. In the light of these considerations, one may hypothesise that where there is no definite objective support in meditation the 'interiorised' body as a whole assumes this essential role.

Concentration is the persistent effort to arrest the natural inclination of the mind to engage in desultory activity, thereby exteriorising itself. Patañjali mentions a series of 'obstacles' (*antarāya*) which impede the cultivation of 'inward-mindedness' (*pratyak-cetanā*). These impediments are sickness, languor, doubt, heedlessness, sloth, dissipation, false vision, the non-attainment of the stages of Yoga and instability in these stages. They are also known as the 'dispersions' (*vikṣepa*)[8] and are said to be accompanied by certain physiological conditions, *viz.* pain, dejection, tremor of the limbs, faulty inhalation and exhalation (see I.33–4). Only by resolute application to single-mindedness can these obstacles and their negative side-effects be overcome (see I.32).

Patañjali knows two synonyms of *dhāraṇā*, *viz. ekāgratā* (III. 11–12) and *ekāgrya*, both meaning 'one-pointedness' (*eka* 'one' + *agra* 'point'). M. Eliade (1973[3], 70) speculated that *ekāgratā* and *dhāraṇā* differ from each other in so far as the latter is a mental fixation for the purpose of comprehension which is absent in *ekāgratā*. I see no evidence for this hypothesis in the *Yoga-Sūtra* itself, though M. Eliade's suggestion is not without interest. As a formal constituent of the eightfold path, *dhāraṇā* is essentially a *technique* which can be said to have as its characteristic feature the one-pointedness of the mind.

We now come to meditative-absorption or *dhyāna*, which, by way of contrast, is defined in III.2 as 'the one-flowness of the presented-ideas'; this is a literal rendering of the Sanskrit compound *pratyaya-ekatānatā*. Implicit in this technical expression is the fact that *dhyāna* is, so to speak, a linear continuation of *ekāgratā* as achieved by the technique of *dhāraṇā*. Yet although meditative-absorption devolves from *dhāraṇā*, it is nevertheless a mental state with its own distinct properties. As T. R. Kulkarni (1972, 119) put it, 'While in *dhāraṇā* the mind remains bound up, as it were, in a restricted space, its continuation in that bound-up state in such a way that the experiential state corresponding to it remains uniformly and homogeneously the same despite variations in the internal or external perceptual situation, constitutes *dhyāna* [. . .] In the state of *dhyāna*, the indeterminateness of perception disappears with the mind remaining unaffected by distracting stimuli.'

J. W. Hauer (1958, 322), who is known to have personally experimented with Yoga, offered this insightful description of the nature of meditative-absorption: '[*Dhyāna*] is a deepened and creative *dhāraṇā*, in which the inner object is illumined mentally. The strict concentration on one object of consciousness is now supplemented with a searching-pensive contemplation of its actual nature. The object is, so to speak, placed before the contemplative consciousness in all its aspects and is apperceived as a whole. Its various characteristics are examined till its very essence is understood and becomes transparent [. . .] This is accompanied by a certain emotive disposition. Although the reasoning faculty functions acutely and clearly, it would be wrong to understand *dhyāna* merely as a logical-rational process: The contemplator must penetrate his object with all his heart, since he is after all primarily interested in a spiritual experience which is to lead him to ontic participation and the emancipation from all constricting and binding hindrances.'

Dhyāna, in other words, adds depth to *dhāraṇā*. Hence G. M. Koelman's (1970) rendering of the term as 'attention' is positively inadequate. *Dhyāna* is not just a prolonged *dhāraṇā*. It must be carefully demarcated from concentration by virtue of its utmost and continuous clarity of consciousness, the relative voidness of the inner space in meditative absorption, the looming large of the single object, the adjustment of all emergent noetic acts to that one object of consciousness, the slow-down of all cognitive and emotive processes and, not least, because of its underpinning of overwhelming peacefulness.[9]

3 *Saṃprajñāta-samādhi*

In *dhyāna* a restructuring of consciousness takes place whose most conspicuous criterion is the increasing proximity between the meditating subject and the object filling the consciousness space. This monoideism brings the *yogin* to a threshold where suddenly and unpredictably consciousness undergoes a further radical reconstruction. This is *samādhi*, the symphysis of subject and object.

The word *samādhi*, composed of *sam* + *ā* + $\sqrt{}$*dhā* 'to put, place', literally means 'putting together'. This does not always come across in the many renderings suggested for this term, such as 'trance' (M. N. Dvivedī, R. Prasāda), 'meditation' (M. Müller, G. Jha), 'concentration' (S. Dasgupta, S. Radhakrishnan, J. H. Woods), 'absorption' (H. Zimmer, G. M. Koelman), 'Versenkung' (E. Frauwallner) and 'Einfaltung' (J. W. Hauer). With the possible exception of the last-mentioned term these transcriptions are either too narrow or too vague to be acceptable.

Hence M. Eliade (1973[3]) borrowed from the Greek language the word 'enstasis' or 'enstasy', which has the advantage of not being loaded with the same kind of unwanted associations that force one to reject the above-mentioned alternatives. For some inexplicable reason this useful coinage has so far not been assimilated into the general technical vocabulary of indologists, and the terminological confusion continues unabatedly. J. Gonda (1960, I, 204) suggested 'identification' as a possible alternative to M. Eliade's unfashionable coinage. But the word 'enstasy' has the additional advantage of clearly demarcating the phenomenon of *samādhi* from that of 'ecstasy', with which it is not infrequently confused.[10] Enstasy, as R. C. Zaehner (1969, 143) observed, 'is the exact reverse of ecstasy, which means to get outside oneself and which is often characterized by a breaking down of the barriers between the individual subject and the universe around him'.

Dhyāna is a necessary, though not a sufficient, condition for *samādhi* to ensue. This all-important point is apodictic from the fact that no genuine volitional acts are possible in meditative-absorption without instantly disrupting the meticulously built up mental continuum. M. Eliade's (1973^3, 80) characterisation of the higher form of enstasy, *i.e. asaṃprajñāta-samādhi*, is in principle also true of any of the lower forms of *samādhi*: '. . . it comes without being summoned, without being provoked, without special preparation for it. That is why it can be called a "raptus" '. *Samādhi* occurs, or rather may occur, when the mind has reached a state of relative equilibrium, that is, when the five types of fluctuations (*vṛtti*) are perfectly restricted (see II.11).

The *Yoga-Sūtra* is quite unequivocal on this, and yet the exegetes have in many ways profoundly upset the conceptual and terminological neatness which makes Patañjali's work such a valuable and appealing document. These distortions are so obtrusive and so symptomatic of the general unreliability of the exegetical literature that I shall for the present purpose abandon my original strategy of altogether ignoring the commentaries as expositional aids. It seems more rewarding to proceed on the basis of a critique of the interpretations or, more precisely, misinterpretations of the classical commentators.

Aphorism III.3 seems an opportune starting-point. Here *samādhi* is characterised in the following way: *tad-eva-artha-mātra-nirbhāsaṃ sva-rūpa-śūnyam-iva samādhiḥ*, '[When] nothing but the object is shining forth [in] that [meditative-absorption], [and when the mind is] as it were void of [its] own-form, [this is known as] enstasy'. Vyāsa, to be sure, understands this *sūtra* quite differently: *dhyānam-eva dhyeya-ākāra-nirbhāsaṃ pratyaya-ātmakena sva-rūpeṇa śūnyam-iva yadā bhavati dhyeya-sva-bhāva-āveśāt-tadā samādhir-ity-ucyate*, 'When meditative-absorption shines forth in the form of the meditated-object (*dhyeya*), as if void of [its] own-form [and being] bodied-forth in presented-ideas, then, on account of [its] fusing with the own-being of the meditated-object, it is called enstasy' (*Yoga-Bhāṣya* III.3).

Vyāsa ostensibly related the words *nirbhāsa* and *sva-rūpa-śūnya* to meditative-absorption and not, as would seem more logical, to the intended object and the mind respectively. But in what sense can *dhyāna* be said to shine forth as the object? And how is one to envisage the loss of its own-form (*sva-rūpa*)? Although Vyāsa's interpretation requires the minimum of filling-in, since he follows tenaciously the overt grammatical structure of the aphorism in question, this is achieved at the cost of intelligibility.

Hence, rather than translating 'that [meditative-absorption] shining-forth *as* the object only', I suggest a reversal, namely 'the object only shining forth *in* that [meditative-absorption]'. Similarly, it would seem to be more cogent to speak of the mind instead of *dhyāna* as being void of its own-form, in view of the fact that in the enstatic condition consciousness, which is normally founded on the dichotomy between subject and object, is deprived of this characteristic dualism. Only in a very loose way could the same be said of *dhyāna*.

In this connection G. Oberhammer (1965, 104, fn. 11) made the curious comment that the fourth stage of *saṃprajñāta-samādhi*, by which he means *asmitā-samādhi*, cannot be determined as *artha-mātra* and *sva-rūpa-śūnya*, since its content is the unity-consciousness of I-am-ness. First of all, as I have shown, there is no such stage of enstasy, and consequently his criticism is unfounded. But even if there were an enstatic state in which all contents of consciousness except the feeling of 'I am' are fully abrogated, still the very fact of the presence of *asmitā* would justify one in describing this enstasy as *artha-mātra* for, to the apperceiving Self (as 'seer' or *draṣṭṛ*), *asmitā* certainly represents an intended object (*artha*).

Furthermore, G. Oberhammer's conjecture that 'coincidence' (*samāpatti*) and 'constraint' (*saṃyama*) pertain to a classification system which is different from that which operates with the concepts of *nirodha* and *saṃprajñāta/asaṃprajñāta-samādhi* is equally untenable. *Samāpatti* is defined in I.41 as follows: *kṣīṇa-vṛtter-abhijātasya-iva maṇer-grahītṛ-grahaṇa-grāhyeṣu tat-stha-tad-añjanatā samāpattiḥ*, '[In the case of the mind whose] fluctuations have dwindled [and which has become] like a transparent-jewel,[11] [there results], [in regard to] the "grasper", the "grasping" and the "grasped", [a state of] coincidence with that on which [the mind] abides and by which [the mind] is "anointed" '.

This *sūtra* describes the basic mechanism of any form of enstasy other than the ultra-cognitive variety (*asaṃprajñāta-samādhi*). Also, I would contend that *samāpatti* is descriptive of the underlying *process* of enstasy whereas *samādhi* is a formal category denoting a *technique*. In other words, the relation between these two terms is analogous to the relation between *ekāgratā* and *dhāraṇā* or between *ekatānatā* and *dhyāna*.

There are four types of *samāpatti* or 'coincidence': *tatra śabda-artha-jñāna-vikalpaiḥ saṃkīrṇa savitarkā samāpattiḥ, smṛti-pariśuddhau sva-rūpa-śūnya-iva-artha-mātra-nirbhāsa nirvitarkā, etayā-eva savicārā nirvicārā ca sūkṣma-viṣayā vyākhyātā* (I.42–4), '[So long as there is] conceptual knowledge [based on] the intent of words in this [*samāpatti*], [it is called] coincidence interspersed with "cogitation". – With the purification of the memory [*i.e.* the tranquilisation of thinking], [when the mind is] as it were void of [its] own-form [and when] the object only shines forth, [this is known as] "ultra-cogitative" [coincidence]. – By these [two types of *samāpatti*] [the other two kinds of coincidence], the "reflexive", and the "ultra-reflexive" [which have] subtle objects [as their meditative support] are explained.'[12]

The cognitive factors present in *vitarka-* and *vicāra-samāpatti* represent a category of mental activity *sui generis* and must not be confused with the fluctuations (*vṛtti*). As is incontestably stated in I.41, enstatic coincidence (*samāpatti*) ensues after the fluctuations have dwindled. Cogitation (*vitarka*) and reflexion (*vicāra*) are specific to the transmuted consciousness in enstasy. They belong to the category of *prajñā* or supra-cognition, *i.e.* gnostic knowledge. As G. M. Koelman (1970, 199) aptly remarked in regard to *vitarka-samādhi*: 'We should not think, however, that a discursive reasoning is going on while one is in the state of "cogitative coarse intentional identity" [. . .] Were it so, there would be no state of absorption, no yogic inhibition of mental activity. Such mental fluctuations are absent, but the immobile intentional identity is in terms of and expressed in rationalizing and conceptualizing signs.' This applies *mutatis mutandis* also to the *vicāra* type of enstatic realisation.

Whereas *vitarka* signifies a supra-cognition in relation to a 'coarse' (*sthūla*) object, that is, anything pertaining to the surface structure of Nature (such as one of the somatic *loci* mentioned by Patañjali or any other micro- or macro-structure of the tangible universe), *vicāra* denotes a supra-cognition in relation to a 'subtle' (*sūkṣma*) object, which can be any phenomenon ranging from the *tanmātras* (see above, pp. 44 f.) up to the transcendental core of the knowable world, *i.e.* the undifferentiate (*aliṅga*). However, in *nirvitarka*- and *nirvicāra-samāpatti* the respective supra-cognitions are fully dispersed and what remains is a consciousness which, like a highly polished mirror, reflects the intended object with a modicum of refraction.

In I.47 it is implied that *nirvicāra-samāpatti* is the highest stage of this series, which suggests the following hierarchic organisation:

nirvicāra-samāpatti
↑
vicāra-samāpatti
↑
nirvitarka-samāpatti
↑
vitarka-samāpatti

There is no mention of any *ānanda-samādhi* or *asmitā-samādhi* in the *Yoga-Sūtra* which would have validated the hypothetical models put forward by Vyāsa, Vācaspati Miśra and their successors. In this context the *Yoga-Bhāṣya* (I.17) contains the following relevant passage: *vitarkaś-cittasya-ālambane sthūla ābhogaḥ sūkṣmo vicāraḥ, ānando hlādaḥ eka-ātmikā saṃvid-asmitā, tatra prathamaś-catuṣṭaya-anugataḥ samādhiḥ savitarkaḥ, dvitīyo vitarka-vikalaḥ savicāraḥ, tṛtīyo vicāra-vikalaḥ sa-ānandaḥ, caturthas-tad-vikalo'smitā-mātra-iti, sarva ete sa-ālambanāḥ samādhayaḥ*, ' "Cogitation" [means] the mind's coarse experience of a [coarse] support; "reflexion" is [the mind's] subtle [experience of a subtle object]; "joy" [means] gladness; "I-am-ness" is the feeling [pertaining] to oneself. Of these [four types] the first, having [all] four associated together, is the enstasy with "cogitation". The second, lacking "cogitation", is [the enstasy] with "reflexion". The third, lacking "reflexion", is [the enstasy] with "joy". The fourth, lacking that ["joy"], is [the enstasy] with [the feeling of] "I-am-ness" only. All these are with supports [*i.e.* intended objects].'

Arranged in a systematic fashion this looks as follows:

asmitā-samādhi	=	*asmitā*
ānanda-samādhi	=	*ānanda* + *asmitā*
vicāra-samādhi	=	*vicāra* + *ānanda* + *asmitā*
vitarka-samādhi	=	*vitarka* + *vicāra* + *ānanda* + *asmitā*

This is a beautiful illustration of the *sat-kārya* axiom according to which the effect is pre-existent in its cause. In this particular case the lowest degree of enstatic realisation contains *in posse* the supra-cognitive elements typical of the higher forms of enstasy. Thus Vyāsa assumes *ānanda* and *asmitā* to constitute the contents of separate stages of *samādhi*. It is unclear how he envisages the correlation between these postulated types and the four varieties of *samāpatti* as cited in I.42–44. Does he take *ānanda-* and *asmitā-samādhi* to be instances of *nirvicāra-samāpatti*? And what sort of experiences do they stand for? Vācaspati Miśra tries to disentangle these knotty problems.

In his *Tattva-Vaiśāradī* (I.17) we find this explanation: *ānanda-iti indriye sthūla-ālambane cittasya-ābhoga āhlādaḥ, prakāśa-śīlāt-tayā khalu sattva-pradhānād-ahaṅkārād-indriyāṇy-utpannāni, sattvaṃ sukham-iti tāny-api sukhāni-iti tasminn-ābhoga āhlāda-iti* (. . .) *asmitā-prabhavāṇi-indriyāṇi, tena-eṣām-asmitā sūkṣmaṃ rūpaṃ, sā ca-ātmanā grahītrā saha buddhir-eka-ātmikā saṃvid-iti*, or 'Joy is the mind's gladdening experience [when directed towards] a sense-organ [which is to be understood as] a coarse support. The sense-organs of course arise from the "I-maker" [in so far as they have] a disposition to enlighten because of the pre-eminence of *sattva* [in them]. [As] *sattva* [manifests] pleasure, these [sense-organs] too are pleasurable. Experience is thus gladdening [when directed towards] those [sense-organs] [. . .] The sense-organs are produced from "I-am-ness"; [consequently] this "I-am-ness" is their subtle form, and this ["I-am-ness"] together with the "grasper" is [known as] *buddhi* [*i.e.*] the feeling [pertaining] to oneself.'

These remarks, not particularly illuminating in themselves, make more sense when viewed in conjunction with Vācaspati Miśra's proposed model of eight types of enstatic coincidence (*samāpatti*). He states (I.46): *tena grāhye catasraḥ samāpattayo grahītṛ-grahaṇayoś-ca catasra ity-aṣṭau te bhavanti-iti*, 'Thus [with regard] to the "grasped" there are four coincidences, [and there are a further] four [in respect to] the "grasper" and "grasping". Thus there are eight of these [coincidences].' Diagrammatically this may be shown as on p. 91.

These conjectural stages of enstatic experience have been admirably analysed by G. M. Koelman (1970, 198 ff.). However, whatever explanatory value they may be credited with, they cannot be reckoned to be representative of Patañjali's viewpoint as reconstructable from the evidence in the *Yoga-Sūtra* itself. At any rate, the profound disagreements between the various exegetes on this crucial issue suffice for us not to accept any of their explanations precipitately.

	objective prop:
nir-asmitā-samāpatti ↑ *asmitā-samāpatti*	'I-am-ness'
↑	
nir-ānanda-samāpatti ↑ *ānanda-samāpatti*	sense-organs
↑	
nir-vicāra-samāpatti ↑ *vicāra-samāpatti*	subtle objects
↑	
nir-vitarka-samāpatti ↑ *vitarka-samāpatti*	coarse objects

While Vācaspati Miśra boldly doubles Vyāsa's perhaps more convincing quartet of enstatic types, Vijñāna Bhikṣu in his *Yoga-Vārttika* (I.46) comes up with a six-stage model. He explicitly rejects Vācaspati Miśra's view according to which the mainstay of *vitarka-* and *vicāra-samādhi* is the internalised object (*grāhya*), of *ānanda-samādhi* the perceptual process (*grahaṇa*) and of *asmitā-samādhi* the category of the Self (*grahītṛ*). Instead he regards 'joy' (*ānanda*) as a product of extreme *vicāra-samāpatti*, which then is made the objective prop of the next higher form of enstasy. *Asmitā-samāpatti*, again, is explained by him as *kevala-puruṣa-ākāra-saṃvid*, that is, the feeling which takes the shape of the transcendental Self. Vijñāna Bhikṣu adamantly denies that there is a *nir-ānanda-* or a *nir-asmitā-samādhi*.

G. M. Koelman (1970) opted for Vācaspati Miśra's interpretation, which he sought to vindicate in what must be considered the most penetrating analysis of this whole problem complex hitherto. However, he was mistaken in his plea that the eight types of *samāpatti* as delineated in the *Tattva-Vaiśāradī* 'are the core of Pātañjala mental discipline' (p. 223). They are indeed 'a magnificent piece of psychology' (*ibid.*), but it remains an open question to what degree this theoretical model is founded on *bona fide* experiential information.

Vācaspati Miśra was undoubtedly a conscientious and extraordinarily erudite scholar, but hardly an initiated *yogin* who could speak authoritatively about such recondite phenomena as these enstatic states. In point of fact, a close inspection of the *Yoga-Sūtra* itself bears out that neither Vācaspati Miśra nor Vijñāna Bhikṣu is a reliable guide in this complicated matter.

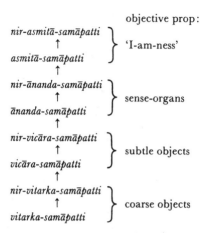

Patañjali's own view seems to be that *nirvicāra-samāpatti* is the highest form of cognitive enstasy (*saṃprajñāta-samādhi*). He states: *nirvicāra-vaiśāradye'dhyātma-prasādaḥ ṛtaṃ-bhārā tatra prajñā* (I.47–48), 'When there is autumnal-lucidity in *nirvicāra*[- *samāpatti*], [then this is called] the clarity of the inner-being. – In this [state of autumnal-lucidity] insight is truth-bearing.'

Vyāsa (I.47) paraphrases this enstatic condition as *bhūta-artha-viṣayaḥ krama-ananurodhī sphuṭa-prajñā-ālokaḥ* or 'the flashing-forth of full-blown (*sphuṭa*) gnosis, not conforming to [the law of] sequence [and having as its] objects the things themselves'. At this culmination of the enstatic process of involution no specific *pratyayas* or 'presented-ideas' remain. There is merely a generic awareness of the essence of the intended object. All noetic acts of the supra-cognitive type (e.g. *vitarka*, etc.) are suspended. Patañjali does not even mention the presence of *ānanda* (meta-bliss) or *asmitā* (meta-subjectivity) in this state, though this need not imply their actual absence.

The gnostic illumination which occurs at this culminant stage is said to be without development. It is, as Vācaspati Miśra (I.47) puts it, 'simultaneous' (*yugapad*), an atemporal knowing which has as its essential characteristic that it is 'truth-bearing' (*ṛtaṃ-bhara*). In other words it is, if one recalls the archaic overtones of the concept of *ṛta*, reflective of the universal order and harmony. This elevated enstatic state is likened to the clarity of the autumnal sky so typical of northern India. The term *vaiśāradya* has its Pāli equivalent in *vesārajja*. It appears that this expression is known in the doctrinal sphere of Buddhism primarily in connection with the teaching of the 'four confidences' (*catvāri vaiśāradyāni*) as, for instance, in the *Bodhisattva-bhūmi* of Asaṇga (U. Wogihara's 1908 ed., p. 402, 1.3 – and his note on p. 39). However, I am reluctant, in the context of Classical Yoga, to translate the term as 'dexterity', as did G. M. Koelman (1970, 226). That it should be given the value of 'lucidity, brightness', etc., is corroborated by virtually all the references to this term in the commentaries, from Vyāsa's *Bhāṣya* to Harihara's nineteenth-century work, which, incidentally, furnishes us with the equation *viśāradī* = *svacchī* or 'transparent' (*ad Yoga-Bhāṣya* II.6).

Of some interest, moreover, is the term *adhyātman* of aphorism I.47, which I have translated as 'inner-being'. It is a key concept in pre-classical Yoga and is explained at length in several passages of the *Mahābhārata* (*viz.* XII.187; 239), especially the *Bhagavad-Gītā* (*viz.* VIII.3, etc.). Reference to it is also made in the *Kaṭha-Upaniṣad*

(II.12; VI.18) and the *Praśna-Upaniṣad* (III.1, 12), but the word is still older, as is borne out by its repeated occurrence in the older Upaniṣads. Basically, it stands for the 'inner world' in its creative-dynamic aspect as *sva-bhāva* ('own-being'), the microcosmic creatrix (*prakṛti*). When its productivity is suspended through Yoga, this is called the 'clarity' (*prasāda*) or 'tranquillity' (*praśānti*) of the inner-being.

In this connection Vyāsa (I.47) cites a stanza identified by Vācaspati Miśra as a *paramā-ṛṣī gāthā*. It reads: *prajñā-prasādam-āruhya aśocyaḥ śocato janān, bhūmi-ṣṭhān-iva śaila-sthaḥ sarvān prajño'nupaśyati*, 'Having ascended to the tranquillity of gnosis, griefless, the man-of-gnosis beholds, like [a person] standing on the mountain[-top] [and looking down upon] the valley-dwellers, all grief-stricken creatures'. This is a popular metaphor which is found in the *Mahābhārata* (XII.17.19; *cf.* Bengali version 151.11),[13] the *Dhammapada* (28), the *Mahāvagga* (I.5, 7), the *Milinda-Pañha* (387) and the *Ahirbudhnya-Saṃhitā* (XV.71–72).

This non-sequential gnosis is further explained in I.49: *śruta-anumāna-prajñābhyām-anya-viṣayā viśeṣa-arthatvāt*, 'The scope [of this gnosis] is distinct from the knowledge [derived from] tradition or inference because of [its] particular purposefulness'. J. H. Woods (1966³) translated this *sūtra* differently: 'Has an object other than the insight resulting from things heard or from inferences inasmuch as its object is a particular.' Although this rendering is true to Vyāsa's diction, who argues that, whilst *śabda* (tradition) and *anumāna* (inference) deal with generic objects only, *samādhi* discloses the particular, nevertheless a far less sophisticated interpretation is possible and also preferable. J. W. Hauer (1958, 337), for instance, understood the phrase *viśeṣa-arthatvāt* as 'weil sein Zweck ein anderer ist', explaining this special purpose to be that of liberation. I find the simplicity of this solution convincing and therefore translate the above phrase 'particular purposefulness'.

The gnostic flash or *prajñā-āloka* spoken of in the *Yoga-Bhāṣya* (I.47) and in the *Yoga-Sūtra* (III.5) can tentatively be understood as the climax of the sevenfold gnosis (*sapta-dhā prajñā*) mentioned in aphorism II.27 (*tasya sapta-dhā prānta-bhūmiḥ prajñā*)[14] and described as arising from the vision of discernment (*viveka-khyāti*, see II.26). A possible elucidation of what might be entailed in this 'sevenfold gnosis' can be found in the *Yoga-Bhāṣya* (II.27): *saptadhā-iti aśuddhy-āvaraṇa-mala-apagamāc-cittasya pratyaya-antara-anutpāde sati sapta-pra-*

kārā-eva prajñā vivekino bhavati, tad-yathā-parijñātaṃ heyaṃ na-asya punaḥ parijñeyam-asti, ksīṇa heya-hetavo na punar-eteṣāṃ kṣetavyam-asti, sākṣāt-kṛtaṃ nirodha-samādhinā hānam, bhavito viveka-khyāti-rūpo hāna-upāyaḥ ity-eṣā catuṣṭayī kāryyā vimuktiḥ prajñāyāḥ, citta-vimuktis-tu trayī carita-adhikārā buddhiḥ guṇā giri-śikhara-kuṭa-cyutā iva grāvāṇo nir-avasthānāḥ, sva-kāraṇe pralaya-abhimukhaḥ saha tena-astaṃ gacchanti, na ca-eṣāṃ pravilīnānāṃ punar-asty-utpādaḥ prayojana-abhāvād-iti, etasyām-avasthāyāṃ-guṇa-sambandha-ātītaḥ sva-rūpa-mātra-jyotir-amalaḥ kevalī puruṣaḥ, ' "Sevenfold" [means that], through the disappearance of the defilements from the cover-of-impurity, when no other presented-idea is produced by the mind, the gnosis of the discerner (*vivekin*) is of seven kinds, [*viz.*] (i) that-which-is-to-be-escaped (*heya*) [*i.e.* all future suffering] is full-comprehended; it need not be full-comprehended again; (ii) the causes of that-which-is-to-be-escaped have dwindled [namely the correlation between "seer" and "seen", etc.]; they need not dwindle again; (iii) through the enstasy of restriction the [total] cessation (*hāna*) is realised; (iv) the means of cessation in the form of the vision of discernment has become manifested; this is the fourfold release of the gnosis to be effected; however, the release of the mind [as such] is triple; (v) the sovereignty of *buddhi* is obtained; (vi) the *guṇas*, like rocks [which have] fallen from the edge of a mountain-peak, are without support [and] of their own accord incline towards dissolution, [and] they go to rest with that [*buddhi*]; and once these [*guṇas*] are dissolved, there is no new origination [for them], because of the absence of the cause [*viz. avidyā* or "nescience"]; (vii) in this state the Self has transcended the connection with the *guṇas* [and is established as] the light of nought but [its] own-form, undefiled [and] alone'.

The vision of discernment (*viveka-khyāti*) is the expedient by which the cessation (*hāna*) of the ominous correlation between Self and non-Self is brought about (see II.26). It is also known as *viveka-ja-jñāna* or 'gnosis born of discernment' (see III.52, 54).[15] Aphorism III.52 is of special interest since it prescribes a method by which this non-sequential gnosis can be effected most directly: *kṣaṇa-tat-kramayoḥ saṃyamād-viveka-jaṃ jñānam*, 'By constraint on the moments-of-time and their sequence [the *yogin* gains] discernment-born gnosis'. The topic of this particular exercise is the structure of time thought to consist of smallest intervals of duration (*kṣaṇa*). In other words, time is made the meditative support by which the atemporal reality is to be actualised.

The commentaries liken these time intervals to the atoms (*parama-aṇu*) of matter, but as I have pointed out above (see p. 49) there is no conclusive evidence for the assumption that Patañjali adopted the atomic conception of matter as developed in the Nyāya and Vaiśeṣika schools of thought. On the other hand, they are probably right in ascribing to him the notion that temporal duration is merely a mental construct (*buddhi-samāhāra*)[16] – a conception not dissimilar to the Kantian conception of time as 'reine Form der sinnlichen Anschauung'.[17] Thus what is real (*vastu*) is the discrete moment (*kṣaṇa*) of the incessant self-transformation of the primary-constituents (*guṇa*) of Nature. It is highly probable that in his metaphysics of time Patañjali was directly inspired by the high-powered speculations of the Sautrāntika Buddhists.

In III.54 this gnostic revelation is described as the 'deliverer' (*tāraka*) owing to its power of transporting the *yogin* across the ocean of phenomenal existence into the Unconditioned. This gnosis is 'omni-objective' (*sarva-viṣaya*), 'omni-temporal' (*sarvatha-viṣaya*) and 'non-sequential' (*akrama*). The quintessence of the vision of discernment is the abolition of the empirical ego. As Patañjali (IV.25) declares, *viśeṣa-darśina ātma-bhāva-bhāvanā-vinivṛttiḥ*, 'For the seer of the distinction [between Self and non-self] [there ensues] the discontinuance of the projection of the self's state'.

The decisive phrase *ātma-bhāva-bhāvanā*, here converted into 'the projection of the self's state', is a problematic one, as is borne out by the existing translations. R. Prasāda (1912), for instance, took it to mean 'the curiosity as to the nature-and-relations of the Self'; G. Jha (1907) proposed 'thought of the nature of self', whilst J. H. Woods (1966³) preferred to translate it as 'pondering upon his own states-of-being'. I submit that these various renderings disregard the active component in *bhāvanā* which is closely allied to *bhāvana*, meaning 'effecting, realising, cultivating'. I therefore propose to translate it as 'projection', which best conveys the element of 'mental construction'.

Supportive evidence for this interpretation is found in Buddhism, where *bhāvanā* is usually given the meaning of 'meditation' or 'visualisation' though, as D. L. Snellgrove (1959, I, 134) pointed out, 'in the special sense of mental production or thought-creation'. Naturally, these considerations apply also to aphorism I.33, which is the only other instance in which the word *bhāvanā* (as *bhāvanātaḥ*) occurs. This *sūtra* is of considerable interest, as it speaks of 'the projecting of friendship, compassion, gladness and impartiality' (*maitrī-*

karuṇā-muditā-upekṣāṇām . . . *bhāvanātaḥ*), which establishes an immediate link with Buddhism, where this set of four mental attitudes is well known and goes under the technical designation of the 'stations of *brahma*' (*brahma-vihāra*).[18]

The term *ātma-bhāva*, again, denotes the empirical self complex which is abolished as soon as *nirvicāra-vaiśāradya* sets in, thus giving way to a state which Vyāsa circumscribes as 'sheer existing' or *sattā-mātra*. The act of 'discernment' (*viveka*) which characterises this enstatic elevation (*prasaṃkhyāna*)[19] is not an ordinary intellectual exercise of 'differentiation' or 'comparison'. Rather it is an immediate knowing (*Innehaben*) of the distinction between Self and self. This explains why the expedient by which the *yogin* propels himself into the next higher stage of enstasy, *viz*. *asaṃprajñāta-samādhi*, is not so much a noetic act as a conative one in the form of a total and irrevocable turning away from prakṛtic reality. I am referring, of course, to *para-vairāgya* or 'higher dispassion' (see III.50; I.16) as the only means of entering into the ultra-cognitive enstasy.

G. M. Koelman (1970, 237) displayed considerable empathic understanding when examining this recondite phenomenon. Trying to determine the nature of this final volition to disengage entirely from *prakṛti* as such, he explained: 'The rejection, however, should not be a violent effort, since this would impair peace of mind. There should be a tranquil suave disinterestedness, a peaceful refraining from thinking, rather than a rejection of the thought of inadequacy or of the thought of otherness, a constant refusal of consciousness and a sinking away into Awareness. The highest state of concentration [*sic*] is, therefore, an effort of the will rather than an activity of the mind.'

4 *Asaṃprajñāta-samādhi*

What happens once the vision of discernment has ceded? The answer is simple: when all conscious contents have been cleared and even the awareness of pure existing is no longer present, consciousness undergoes a total collapse. There is a gradual emptying of consciousness in the course of the enstatic journey, and then comes the critical point at which 'implosion' occurs owing to the extreme evacuation of the mind. This is *asaṃprajñāta-samādhi*, which coincides with the restriction of all presented-ideas (*pratyaya-nirodha*).

However, this absence of consciousness does not mean that the ultra-cognitive enstasy is equivalent to a state of unconsciousness as ordinarily understood. Such an interpretation is not defensible on any count, since Yoga is careful to differentiate between consciousness (*citta*) and Awareness (*cit*).[20] For this reason one must also reject G. Jha's (1907) translation of the term *asaṃprajñāta* as 'unconscious'. A somewhat more appropriate rendering would appear to be 'ultra-cognitive' as suggested by M. N. Dvivedī (1943[3]). As S. Dasgupta (1924, 124) commented, 'This state, like the other previous states of the saṃprajñāta type, is a positive state of the mind and not a mere state of vacuity of objects or negativity. In this state, all determinate character of the states disappears and their potencies only remain alive.' G. M. Koelman (1970, 239), more punctiliously perhaps, put it thus: 'Concentration [*sic*] without objective consciousness should not be conceived as total absence of knowledge; only knowledge by objectivation is absent'.

This rather elusive condition is also called 'restriction transformation' (*nirodha-pariṇāma*) in aphorism III.9: *vyutthāna-nirodha-saṃskārayor-abhibhava-prādur-bhāvau nirodha-kṣaṇa-citta-anvayo nirodha-pariṇamaḥ*, '[When there is] subjugation of the subliminal-activators of emergence and the manifestation [of the subliminal-activators] of restriction [this is known as] the restriction transmutation [or] the connection of consciousness with the moment of restriction'. The immediately succeeding aphorism (III.10) complements this statement: *tasya praśānta-vāhitā saṃskārāt*, 'Its calm flow [is effected] by a subliminal-activator'.

The specialness of the restriction transformation (*nirodha-pariṇāma*) is brought out by aphorisms III.11–12, which define the other non-ordinary 'transmutations' (*pariṇāma*) of the mind: *sarva-arthatā-ekāgratayoḥ kṣaya-udayau cittasya samādhi-pariṇāmaḥ, tataḥ punaḥ śānta-uditau tulya-pratyayau cittasya ekāgratā-pariṇāmaḥ*, 'The dwindling of all-object-ness and the uprisal of one-pointedness is the enstasy transmutation of the mind. – Then again, when the quiescent and the uprisen presented-ideas are similar, [this is] the one-pointedness transmutation of the mind.' Whereas III.12 is seemingly a description of the underlying process of the techniques of *dhāraṇā* and *dhyāna*, aphorism III.11 refers to the central happening in enstasy.

The term *sarva-arthatā*, which occurs only in III.11, is decisive. Contrary to the contention of the classical exegetes, who equate this expression with *viṣaya* or external object, *arthatā* must be taken to denote 'intended object'. Nor can I accept S. Dasgupta's (1924, 155) interpretation of III.9 that '[e]ven when the mind is in the saṃprajñāta state it is said to be in vyutthāna (phenomenal) in comparison with the nirodha state, just as the ordinary conscious states are called vyutthāna in comparison with the samprajñāta state'. Evidently he read slightly more into this aphorism than is actually there. It seems to me that the term *vyutthāna* merely qualifies the term *saṃskāra* and is not applied to the enstatic condition as such.

From the viewpoint of the empirical consciousness, the ultra-cognitive enstasy (*asaṃprajñāta-samādhi*) is but a mass of subliminal-activators (see I.18) which devour each other step-by-step because they are prevented from conscious thematisation and also because there is no further feedback from consciousness. This state is also designated as 'seedless' (*nir-bīja*, III.8) in contrast to the *sa-bīja* forms of *samāpatti*. The word *bīja* or 'seed' refers either to the 'support' (*ālambana*), *i.e.* the intended object, or the subliminal-activators (see above, pp. 67 ff.).

Initially, *asaṃprajñāta-samādhi* is only a fleeting experience intercalating itself into the general enstatic continuum on the level of *saṃprajñāta-samādhi*. For by dint of the subliminal tensions the *yogin* reverts again and again to the lower forms of enstatic experience (see IV.27). Nonetheless, once the utmost boundary of the ultra-reflexive coincidence (*nirvicāra-samāpatti*) is reached, he is carried as if by a powerful current towards *kaivalya* (see IV.26). This is so because, despite the innumerable *vāsanās*, Nature ultimately serves the end of the Self (see IV.24).

5 *Dharma-megha-samādhi*

The concept of *dharma-megha-samādhi* makes its appearance in a single aphorism, namely IV.29, which reads as follows: *prasaṃkhyāne'py-akusīdasya sarvathā viveka-khyāter-dharma-meghaḥ samādhiḥ*, 'For [the *yogin* who is] always non-usurious (*a-ku-sīda*) even in [the state of] enstatic-elevation (*prasaṃkhyāna*) [there follows] from the vision of discernment the enstasy [known as] the cloud of *dharma*'. The word *akusīda* describes the adept who applies himself to the higher form of dispassion or *para-vairāgya* by which the ultra-cognitive enstasy (*asaṃprajñāta-samādhi*) is realised. The term *dharma-megha-samādhi* can be either a straightforward synonym of *asaṃprajñāta-samādhi* or, else, refers to the consummate phase of this highest type of enstasy. I shall argue in favour of the second alternative.

This important concept is surrounded by a certain enigma which the classical commentators have failed to illuminate, as is clearly evinced by their contradictory and occasionally even self-contradictory interpretations of the precise location of *dharma-megha-samādhi* within the whole series of enstatic experiences. In his *Yoga-Bhāṣya* (I.2) Vyāsa makes the following statement: *tad-eva rajo-leśa-mala-apetaṃ sva-rūpa-pratiṣṭhaṃ sattva-puruṣa-anyatā-khyāti-mātraṃ dharma-megha-dhyāna-upagaṃ bhavati, tat-paraṃ prasaṃkhyānam-ity-ācakṣate dhyāyinaḥ*, '[When] the defilement of the vestiges of *rajas* is removed from that [state of *sattva*] [and when consciousness] is grounded in [its] own-form [and is] nothing but the vision of the distinction between Self and *sattva*, [then] it tends towards the absorption [known as] the cloud of *dharma*; that [*sattva* state is designated by meditators as the supreme enstatic-elevation'.

In his voluminous *Yoga-Vārttika* (I.2) Vijñāna Bhikṣu explains this passage thus: *dharma-megha-dhyānaṃ kim-ity-ākāṅkṣa-ayam-āha tat-param-iti tad-dharma-megha-ākhyāṃ dhyānaṃ paramaṃ prasaṃkhyānaṃ tattva-jñānaṃ viveka-khyāter-eva*, 'What is the absorption [known as] the cloud of *dharma*? Anticipating this query [Vyāsa] says: "that is the supreme [enstatic-elevation]". That absorption called the "cloud of *dharma*" is the supreme enstatic-elevation, true knowledge [born of] the vision of discernment.' Clearly, this is a gross misconstruction of Vyāsa's stance. As is evident from subsequent statements in the *Yoga-Bhāṣya* (see I.15; II.2; IV.29) the author does not identify *prasaṃkhyāna* with *dharma-megha-samādhi*, and consequently the word *tad* ('that') in the last sentence of the above quotation does not refer to *dharma-megha-dhyāna* (= °-*samādhi*),[21] as Vijñāna Bhikṣu maintains, but to the state of unpolluted *sattva*.

G. M. Koelman (1970, 234) regarded *dharma-megha-samādhi* as the 'passage from the state of Sublime Insight to the state of Restriction', that is, from *prasaṃkhyāna* to *asaṃprajñāta-samādhi*. He contended (p. 235) that the 'enstasy of the cloud of *dharma*' 'is the stage where there is absolutely uninterrupted discriminate intuition, at once apprehended and generously sacrificed, an uninterrupted experience of the fact that in our present state we do not square with our true Self . . .'. But this is neither the view of Patañjali nor that of Vyāsa.

G. M. Koelman (1970) tried to vindicate his interpretation by citing Vācaspati Miśra (I.18): *dharma-megha-samādhi-eva hi nitānta-vigalita-rajas-tamo-malāt-sattvad-upajātas-tat-tad-viṣaya-atikrameṇa pra-*

varttamāno'nanto viṣaya-avadyadarśī samasta-viṣaya-parityāgāc-ca sva-rūpa-pratiṣṭhaḥ san-nirālambanaḥ saṃskāra-mātra-śeṣasya nirālambanasya samādheḥ kāraṇam-upapadyate sārūpyād, 'When *sattva* is entirely freed from the defilements of *rajas* and *tamas*, the *dharma-megha* enstasy is effected. Its activity is transcendent to any object. [It is] unbounded, beholding [all] objects and on account of [the mind's] shunning of all objects [it remains] grounded in [its] own-form, being without support. It acts as the cause of the enstasy [which has] only a vestige of subliminal-activators [and which is] without support owing to [its] homogeneity.'

This exposition goes, probably unintentionally, against all the evidence in the *Yoga-Sūtra* and also against the authority of Vyāsa. For instance, in IV.30 it is stated that 'thence [*i.e.* as a result of *dharma-megha-samādhi*] [comes about] the cessation of [all] causes-of-affliction and of *karman*' (*tataḥ kleśa-karma-nivṛttiḥ*). This interpretation is reinforced by the whole context of the concluding *sūtras*, in which the concept of *dharma-megha-samādhi* is first introduced. Accordingly, one is forced to conclude that the *dharma-megha* enstasy forms the terminal stage of *asaṃprajñāta-samādhi* and that it coincides with the *yogin*'s exit from the prakṛtic realm *in toto*. For this reason one must also discard the equation, proposed in the *Pātañjala-Rahasya* (IV.29), of *dharma-megha-samādhi* with the higher renunciation (*para-vairāgya*). Strictly speaking, *para-vairāgya* serves as the *means* to *asaṃprajñāta-samādhi*.

Having clarified the position of this puzzling phenomenon on the enstatic *scala*, it remains to ascertain the meaning of the concept of *dharma* in *dharma-megha*. The older generation of indologists have focused on the ethical connotation of this polysemous word and invariable translated it with 'virtue' (G. Jha, R. Prasāda, M. Müller) or 'merit' (M. N. Dvivedī).[22] More recent researchers have found these renderings unsatisfactory and, tacitly or openly, queried that *dharma* in the present context has a moral sense.[23] Thus S. Radhakrishnan (1951^6) rendered it as 'truth', G. M. Koelman (1970) as 'essence' and J. H. Woods (1966^3) suggested '[knowable] thing', whilst J. W. Hauer (1958), taking his cue from buddhist contexts, understood it as 'tragende Urmacht'. Explaining this unexpected paraphrase, J. W. Hauer (p. 470, fn. 22) wrote: 'The meditator is in this state enveloped by the supporting primal power (*tragende Urmacht*) of the world; he has become a *dharmakāya* like the "great Muni". This is an expression for the Buddha who has entered Nirvāṇa.'

I find this interpretation persuasive. For the concept of *dharma-megha* does not appear to be mentioned by any hindu authority prior to Patañjali, though it is evidently an integral part of the technical nomenclature of early Mahāyāna Buddhism.[24] There it figures as the tenth *bhūmi* or 'stage' of the *bodhisattva*'s path to perfection, as can be seen, for example, from the *Pañcaviṃśati-Sāhasrikā-Prajñāpāramitā* (p. 230, ed. by N. Dutt, 1934). It is my contention that Patañjali was well aware of these doctrinal elaborations of post-Christian Buddhism. This raises anew the vexed question, broached by previous scholars (*e.g.* L. de la Vallée Poussin, 1936–37), of the exact relation between Classical Yoga and Buddhism.[25]

6 *Saṃyama and the siddhis*

This section takes us a step back as it were from the ultimate goal of Self-realisation as heralded by the ultra-cognitive enstasy of the 'cloud of *dharma*'. The withdrawal of consciousness from the external world transmitted *via* the senses, and its interiorisation and localisation by means of the practice of concentration, meditation and, finally enstasy, opens up a new dimension of reality. The *yogin* gains access to a unique form of experiencing and knowledge which restructures his entire being. This is sometimes described in terms of the formation of a new, 'subtle' body with its own peculiar organs and capabilities. The accomplished *yogin* is thought to be endowed with extraordinary powers, known as the *siddhis*, which 'obsess Indian mythology, folklore and metaphysics with equal intensity'.[26] What are these paranormal attainments which no yogic text fails to mention?

In his treatment of the philosophy of Classical Yoga according to the exegeses in the commentaries, S. Dasgupta (1924, 157 f.) dealt with the question of the powers summarily in fifteen lines and a single table. This reflects well the consensus of scholarly opinion, according to which the supernatural attainments are discordant with Patañjali's rational approach and his philosophical objectives. However, the fact is that one sixth of the aphorisms concerns precisely this recondite aspect of Yoga, and one chapter of the vulgate is actually entitled *vibhūti-pāda*. How can we account for this obvious pre-eminence given to the 'magical' side of the yogic path? Was Patañjali, after all, not such a staunch rationalist as contemporary interpreters have made him out to be? Has he perhaps unwittingly succumbed to the magical trend in Yoga, betraying its putative shamanistic origins?

These questions can all be instantly disposed of by the simple observation that the powers form an integral part of all yogic endeavour. This was first distinctly and clearly articulated by P. V. Kane (1962, 1452 ff.) and was later reaffirmed by J. W. Hauer (1958, 324 ff.) and, independently, by M. Eliade (1973[3], 85 ff., 177 ff.). More recently C. Pensa (1969) has given the matter more serious attention. He summarised his review of the problem as follows: '. . . the "power" element, implicit or explicit as it may be, is intrinsic to the very structure of Yoga, in close correlation with the concepts of purification and knowledge [. . .] Each implies and is implicit in the other: progress in one means progress in the others, nor could any progress be thinkable outside this organic interaction' (p. 21). Furthermore: 'As to the "powers" or "perfections" (*vibhūtis*, *siddhis*), they are no other [. . .] than specializations of this power [. . .] In consequence, neither power nor "the powers", if we want to make this distinction, can be in any way separated from Yoga's essentially organic and unitary structure; considering them as spurious elements or magical residues has no textual basis' (p. 22).

Notwithstanding the use of the word *vibhūti* in the title of the third chapter, Patañjali only mentions the term *siddhi* in the actual text. Occurring four times in the *Yoga-Sūtra*, only in one instance (*viz.* IV.1) does the word *siddhi* unequivocally denote the supranormal powers. The aphorism in question states that they are procurable by herbal concoctions (*oṣadhi*), spells (*mantra*), austerities (*tapas*), enstasy (*samādhi*) or are the result of an innate aptitude (*janman*). However, textual criticism has shown this *sūtra* to be a later interpolation.[27] In II.43 the word has the meaning of 'perfection'; in II.45 the compound *samādhi-siddhi* can mean either 'perfection of enstasy' or, more radically interpreted, 'attainment of enstasy'. Lastly, in the much misunderstood aphorism III.37, it is probably also employed in a non-technical sense (as 'attainment').

The word *vibhūti* has a long history. It was first used as an adjective in the *Ṛgveda* (*viz.* I.8.9; 30.5; VI.21.1, etc.) signifying 'extensive, abundant, mighty', and corresponding with the later expression *vibhūtimat*. In classical Sanskrit the word functions primarily as a feminine substantive meaning 'development, power, magnificence, prosperity', etc. In the tenth chapter of the *Bhagavad-Gītā*, entitled *vibhūti-yoga*, Kṛṣṇa speaks of his 'powers-of-manifestation' (*vibhūti*) and his Yoga (X.7).[28] In X.16 and 19 the compound *ātma-vibhūtayaḥ* occurs, which can be rendered as 'Self's powers-of-manifestation'. Verses 19 *et seq.* tell us what precisely Kṛṣṇa's powers *in excelsior* are. Thus we learn that he is *meru* among mountains (vs. 23), the syllable *oṃ* among all sounds (vs. 25), the sage Nārada among all the seers (vs. 26), Kapila among the perfected-ones (*siddha*) (vs. 26), Self-knowledge among all kinds of knowledge (vs. 32), Vyāsa among all the silent-sages (*muni*) (vs. 37), etc.

As W. D. P. Hill (1966², 148, fn. 4) noted long ago, the word *vibhūti* 'contains an idea of "power" or "lordship" and also an idea of "pervasion" or "immanence" '. He sought to capture this dual aspect by translating the term as 'pervading power'. In regard to the *Yoga-Sūtra*, the first connotation appears to be the more pertinent of the two, conveying more or less the same ideas as the term *siddhi*. There is an interesting passage in the *Prapañcasāra-Vivaraṇavyākhyā*[29] in which the relation between these two terms is determined as follows: *paramaṃ vibhūti-kāṣṭhāṃ prāpta-iti siddhi-lakṣaṇo hetuḥ, para-kaivalya-siddhi-paryantāṃ vibhūtim-iti bhāvaḥ*, ' "Having reached the supreme limit of power" [means] the condition relating to the *siddhis*. [It is] "the power terminating in the supreme *siddhi* of aloneness (*kaivalya*)".' Although written many centuries after the composition of the *Yoga-Sūtra*, these lines are not unrepresentative of earlier usage.

The paranormal attainments of Yoga can be grouped into two broad categories, *viz.* mental and physical or quasi-physical powers. The first entail the acquisition of a special kind of knowledge (*jñāna*), the latter such abilities as levitation, telekinesis, etc. Some phenomena, however, straddle both these categories, as, for instance, the *yogin*'s unwitting harmonising influence on his environment (II.35). Another possible way of classifying these non-ordinary attainments would be according to their putative causes. Here we can distinguish paranormal achievements procured by following (1) the moral code of Yoga (i.e. *yama* and *niyama*), (2) the practice of posture (*āsana*), breath-control (*prāṇāyāma*), and sense-withdrawal (*pratyāhāra*) and (3) by the application of enstatic constraint (*saṃyama*).

To the reader of the New Testament the ideal that moral perfection should yield a certain power is not surprising. The *Yoga-Sūtra* details the supranormal gain for each of the practices of restraint (*yama*) and observance (*niyama*). Thus the yogin's grounding in the virtue of non-harming (*ahiṃsā*) is said to have a positive impact on his surroundings, with the effect that in his immediate vicinity all feelings of enmity are blocked (II.35). His accomplishment in truthfulness (*satya*) makes his every word come true (II.36). The *yogin* who has mastered the virtue of non-stealing (*asteya*), understood in a more comprehensive sense than usual, wins all kinds of jewels (II.37), which is probably to be interpreted metaphorically. Again, chastity (*brahmacarya*) practised to perfection leads to the vitality (*vīrya*) necessary for the great spiritual struggle which lies ahead (II.38). Perfect greedlessness (*aparigraha*), the last of the five constituents of *yama*, brings him insight into the wherefore of his birth (II.39).

Through purity (*śauca*) he acquires distance from the body[30] and the need and ability not to mix with others so as not to be 'contaminated', *i.e.* morally polluted, by them (II.40). This is also said to bring about purity of the *sattva*, gladness, one-pointedness, mastery of the senses and the capability of Self-vision[31] (II.41). Contentment (*saṃtoṣa*), again, confers unexcelled joy on him (II.42). From austerity (*tapas*), which presumably consists in such practices as fasting or observing complete silence, he gains perfection of the body and the senses (II.43). Self-study (*svādhyāya*) bring him into contact with his chosen deity (II.44), and devotion to the Lord (*īśvara-praṇidhāna*) is the means of attaining, or perfecting, enstasy (II.45).

Mastery of posture (*āsana*) immunises the *yogin* against the impact of the pairs-of-opposites (*dvandva*), like heat and cold, humidity and aridity, etc. (II.48). Breath-control (*prāṇāyāma*) removes the covering concealing the inner light (II.52) and thus makes the mind fit for concentration (II.53). Through accomplishment in sense-withdrawal (*pratyāhāra*) he effects the full subjugation of the senses (II.55). Mastery of the up-breath (*udāna*) gives him the ability to extract himself from thorns or mud and to rise from the water (III.39). Mastery of the mid-breath (*samāna*), again, induces *prajvalana* or 'effulgence', which Vyāsa understands as the kindling of the bodily heat.

Next we come to the diverse products of the practice of constraint (*saṃyama*), whose primary target is the flashing-forth of transcendental-insight (*prajñā-āloka*) (III.5). *Saṃyama* is, in fact, the *via regia* of Yoga. In the epic (*e.g.* XII.266.15) this term is still used loosely and generally in connection with the control of the sensory apparatus, but in Classical Yoga it figures as a technical expression of the first order. It denotes the conjoint practice of concentration, meditative-absorption and enstasy with regard to a single object. Since, paradoxically, the Unconditioned and Formless, *i.e.* the Self, can only be reached *via* the manifest forms, the yogic journey *volens nolens* takes the adept through the depths of cognitive-enstasy (*saṃprajñāta-samādhi*) and thus inevitably confronts him also with the mysteries of the powers (*siddhi*) arising from these special states of consciousness.

In aphorism I.40 it is clearly enunciated that by virtue of the stalwart practice of meditative-absorption, leading to enstasy, everything from the most minute to the very largest comes under the *yogin*'s control.[32] This is also known as the supremacy over all states-of-existence (*sarva-bhāva-adhiṣṭhātṛtva*) (III.49). Coterminous with this unlimited lordship over the cosmos is his omniscience (*sarva-jñātṛtva*) (III.49). Both are the fruit of that highest form of cognitive enstasy which consists merely in the uninterrupted discernment of the difference between Self and *sattva*. Knowledge born of discernment (*viveka-ja-jñāna*) is the outcome of constraint upon the atoms-of-time (*kṣaṇa*) and their sequence (III.52). From this is said to result *pratipatti*, paraphrased by Vijñāna Bhikṣu as *sākṣātkāra* or 'immediate-perception'.

From constraint upon the three kinds of transformation (*pariṇāma*)[33] knowledge of the past and future is acquired (III.16). The ability to understand the sounds of all beings is obtained through constraint upon the difference between the object, its representation in consciousness and its linguistic label (III.17). Knowledge of previous existences comes about through the direct-perception (*sākṣātkāra*), again in the enstatic state, of the respective subliminal-activators (III.18). When the ideas in the mind of another person are made the subject of constraint, the *yogin* gains knowledge of that mind (III.19) but not, as Patañjali specifically points out, of the underlying object of those mental representations (III.20). Knowledge of imminent death is obtained through constraint upon *karman* (III.22), which presumably involves processes similar to those of III.18. By focusing (*nyāsa*) the flashing-forth of those mental activities (*pravṛtti*) which are sorrowless and illuminating (see I.35–36), the adept acquires knowledge of the subtle, the hidden and the distant (III.25). The experience referred to in this aphorism remains somewhat obscure, but Vijñāna Bhikṣu correctly takes *nyāsa* to be synonymous with *saṃyama*.

Knowledge of the structure of the universe comes about through the practice of constraint upon the sun (III.26). Knowledge of the movement of the seemingly stationary pole-star comes from constraint upon it (III.28). Knowledge of the arrangement of the stars is gained from constraint upon the moon (III.27). The structure of the body is disclosed through constraint upon the 'navel wheel' (*nābhi-cakra*) (III.29). Through constraint upon the 'throat well' (*kaṇṭha-kūpa*), hunger and thirst are conquered (III.30). Rock-like stability (*sthairya*) is the by-product of constraint upon the 'tortoise tube' (*kūrma-nāḍī*). The subtle physiology of *cakras* and *nāḍīs* belongs to the archaic stock of yogic ideas, and hence their mention in Patañjali's work need not signify the impact of Tantrism on Classical Yoga. Incidentally, Patañjali does not refer to the *kuṇḍalinī-śakti* or 'serpent power', which appears to have been unknown to him. This conception was first formulated by the tantric *ācāryas* of the period after Vyāsa.[34]

Enstatic focusing upon the 'light in the head' (*mūrdha-jyotis*) brings about the vision of the perfected-ones (*siddha*) (III.32). When there is a sudden flash-of-illumination (*prātibha*) in the enstatic condition, the *yogin* beholds everything (*sarva*) with his mental eye (III.33). Through constraint upon the heart, he obtains understanding (*saṃvid*) of the nature of consciousness (III.34). Self-knowledge (*puruṣa-jñāna*), again, comes about through constraint upon the particular purpose of the Self and Nature respectively (III.35).

In the course of his enstatic endeavours, he also meets with flashes-of-illumination in the sphere of the senses (III.36), which probably means that he becomes clairvoyant, clairaudient, etc. These are the phenomena hinted at already in the *Śvetāśvatara-Upaniṣad* (II.11–12): *nīhāra-dhūma-arka-anila-analānāṃ khadyota-vidyut-sphaṭika-śaśīnām, etāni rūpāṇi puraḥ-sarāṇi brahmaṇy-abhivyaktikarāṇi yoge; pṛthivy-ap-tejo'nila-khe samuthite pañca-ātmake yoga-guṇe pravṛtte, na tasya rogo na jarā na mṛtyuḥ prāptasya yoga-agni-mayaṃ śarīram*, 'The forms preceding and causing the manifestation of *brahman* in Yoga are [like] mist, smoke, the sun, fire, wind, firefly (*kha-dyota*), lightning, crystal or the moon. – When the fivefold qualities of Yoga, arising from the [element of] earth, water, fire, wind and ether, have come-into-activity [then the yogin who] has obtained a body made of the fire of Yoga does not [experience] illness, old age or death.'

These phenomena, Patañjali explains (III.37), are perfections/powers (*siddhi*) in the waking state, but obstacles in enstasy. It is neither necessary nor justifiable to generalise this statement to include all paranormal phenomena, as did M. Eliade (1973[3], 90) and others. For instance, the knowledge gained from constraint upon the pole-star is not in any way distinct from the enstatic condition itself but constitutes its essence. This is different in the case of the supra-sensory flashes-of-illumination which involve the externalisation of consciousness. However, like all sensory processes, even these para-normal ways of sensing must be checked to recover the enstatic state.

In addition to these cognitive attainments, the *yogin* also gains access to powers or abilities of a para-physical nature. Through constraint upon the virtue of friendliness (*maitrī*) and the other three 'infinitudes' (see p. 95) he acquires great strength (*bala*) (III.23). And if he makes particular manifestations of strength, like that of the elephant, the subject of his enstasy, he secures for himself the strength of an elephant, etc. (III.24). Constraint upon the relation between ear and ether leads to the 'divine ear' (*divya-śrota*) (III.41). When the topic of his enstatic focusing is the relation between body and ether, he wins the ability to traverse the ether (*ākāśa-gamana*), which may be interpreted literally (as levitation) or as 'astral-projection'.

A related phenomenon is referred to in III.38, which speaks of the mental penetration of another body. Also, aphorism III.43 may be pertinent where a non-imaginary fluctuation (*akalpita-vṛtti*) outside the body is mentioned which, when realised, removes the covering the inner light. Mastery of the elements (*bhūta*) results from the practice of constraint upon their various levels of manifestation (III.44). At this point the *yogin* obtains the eight classic powers of atomisation (*aṇimān*), magnification (*mahimān*), levitation (*laghimān*), limitless-extension (*prāpti*), freedom-of-will (*prākāmya*), mastery-of-creation (*vaśitva*), lordship (*īśitṛtva*) and wish fulfillment (*kāmā-vasāyitva*). He also acquires bodily perfection (*kāya-saṃpad*) and physical indestructibility (*anabhighāta*) (III.45). Mastery of the senses, again, comes about through constraint upon their various levels of manifestation (III.47). It further results in the ability to move about at the speed of the mind (*mano-javitva*), and the mastery of the foundation of Nature itself (III.48). The power of making himself invisible (*antardhāna*) comes as a result of constraint upon the structure of the human body (III.21).

The Yoga adept is thus not only the possessor of a special kind of knowledge, but is also endowed with special physical or quasi-physical abilities. Yet more important than either of these excellences is his possession of himself, in the form of the actualisation of his true Self. The powers are the inevitable by-products of his prolonged struggle towards this lofty goal. They cannot be separated from the profound transformation which he has to undergo in order to realise the Self. Viewed differently again, they are signposts along the way or, in contemporary parlance, confirmative evidence that he is on the right track.

They can but strengthen the *yogin*'s faith (*śraddhā*) in the efficacy of Yoga and spurn him on. I believe Vācaspati Miśra to be basically right in his claim that 'the powers (*vibhūti*) are not quite uninstrumental [in the attainment] of aloneness; however, [they are] not directly [the causes of emancipation]' (*na-atyantam-ahetavaḥ kaivalye vibhūtayaḥ kin-tu na sākṣād*). Nevertheless, his contention that the vision of discernment (*viveka-khyāti*) is to be regarded as the real and principal cause is unacceptable. Strictly speaking, emancipation is uncaused, for it is the permanent essence of the Self. Consequently, his distinction between actual and figurative causes makes little sense. The powers are as much or as little productive of liberation as are the gnostic insights. Both are two aspects of the same complex process of total transmutation of the finite personality leading to the recovery of the ever free transcendental Self.

VII
Pātañjala Yoga and Classical Sāṃkhya

Of the plethora of misrepresentations of Patañjali's *darśana*, both by foreign and indigenous scholars, none proved more inveterate and damaging than the claim that Classical Yoga is but a *Spielart* of Sāṃkhya. This infelicitous assumption was first proposed by H. T. Colebrooke in his now classical essay on Yoga.[1] According to him there is but a single difference between Yoga and Sāṃkhya, namely the affirmation of the doctrine of *īśvara* by the former and its denial by the latter school of thought. 'In less momentous matters they differ, not upon points of doctrine, but in the degree in which the exterior exercises, or abstruse reasoning and study, are weighed upon, as requisite preparations of absorbed contemplation.'[2] This mistaken view was destined to be echoed and re-echoed throughout the next century. The following statements, culled almost at random from the indological literature, are symptomatic of this fundamental misapprehension, and its ghost is to be found haunting the pages even of quite recent publications.

In the same vein as H. T. Colebrooke, R. Mitra (1883, xviii) wrote: 'The Yoga Sutra takes for granted the twenty-five categories of the Sánkhya as the basis of its doctrine, and copies some of its aphorisms almost *verbatim*.' Similarly M. N. Dvivedī (1890, 1943³, xviii): 'The *Yoga* subscribes to the *Sāṃkhya* theory in *toto*.' M. Monier-Williams (1894, 200), again, stated: 'The Yoga, founded by Patanjali and regarded as a branch of the Sānkhya, is scarcely worthy of the name of a separate system of philosophy. Yet it has undoubted charms for the naturally contemplative and ascetical Hindū . . .'

Although correcting some of the mistaken notions about Yoga and displaying a far more liberal-minded attitude towards it than did his predecessors, M. Müller (1916⁴, 312) nonetheless followed suit when claiming: '. . . it may be quite true that, after we have once understood the position of the Sāmkhya-philosophy towards the great problem of the world, we shall not glean many new metaphysical or psychological ideas from a study of the Yoga'. R. Garbe (1917[2], 148), well known for his pioneer work on Sāṃkhya, made no concessions to Yoga at all: 'All Sāṃkhya teachings about cosmology, physiology and psychology were simply taken over into the Yoga system. Even the doctrine of salvation is the same . . .' S. Radhakrishnan (1927, 1951[6], II, 342) expressed a more moderate but still not affirmative enough view: 'Patañjali systematised the conceptions of the Yoga and set them forth on the background of the metaphysics of the Sāṃkhya, which he assumes with slight variations'.

The first scholar to come to the defence of Classical Yoga and vigorously affirm its doctrinal autonomy was S. Dasgupta (1930, 2) who, seeking to rectify past misinterpretations and sweeping generalisations, observed: 'It is true that Yoga owes much to the Sāṅkhya philosophy, but it is doubtful whether the obligation is due to the Kapila Sāṅkhya as we have it now. My supposition is that we have lost the original Sāṅkhya texts, whereas the systems that pass now by the name of Sāṅkhya and Yoga represent two schools of philosophy which evolved through the modifications of the original Sāṅkhya school; Yoga did not borrow its material from Kapila Sāṅkhya [. . .] though the Yoga and the Kapila Sāṅkhya are fundamentally the same in their general metaphysical positions, yet they hold quite different views on many points of philosophical, ethical and practical interest.'

M. Eliade (1973[3], 7), a former student of S. Dasgupta, regrettably blurred this fine distinction again when stating: 'As to the theoretical framework and the metaphysical foundation that Patañjali provides for these practices, his personal contribution is of the smallest. He merely rehandles the Sāṃkhya philosophy in its broad outlines, adapting it to a rather superficial theism in which he exalts the practical value of meditation. The Yoga and Sāṃkhya systems are so much alike that most of the affirmations made by the one are valid for the other.'

A more discerning view was put forward by F. Catalina (1968, 19): 'In the main, the two systems are very much alike. However, there are some significant differences which warrant our calling Yoga a separate system of philosophy.' This enlightened position has unfortunately not become as widely prevalent as one would wish. Too often Yoga is still being reduced to Sāṃkhya, occasionally credited with a few unimportant appendages of its own. For instance, C. Sharma (1960, 169) made this indefensible comment: 'Yoga is intimately allied to Sāṅkhya. The Gītā calls them one. Yoga means spiritual action and Sāṅkhya means knowledge. Sāṅkhya is theory; Yoga is practice. For all practical purposes, Sāṅkhya and Yoga may be treated as the theoretical and the practical sides of the same system.'

However, as a perusal of the literature quickly evinces, it is not only Indian scholars who are guilty of this kind of reductionism and over-generalisation. N. Smart (1968, 26), for example, wrote: 'The Samkhya system can hardly by itself be treated as a method of liberation, though it lays claim to being such, which is a main reason why it is coupled, and has been coupled over a very long period, with the Yoga system. The latter borrows its main features, with certain adaptations, from the Samkhya, so that it is not too misleading to treat Samkhya as the theoretical exposition and Yoga the practical account of how to achieve that clarity of consciousness which brings liberation from the round of rebirth and the suffering of the world.'

Such inept statements could be multiplied almost *ad libitum*. They all betray a certain lack of historical perspective which, in turn, is responsible for an almost incredible conceptual haziness. It is futile to attempt a comparison between two items which have not been clearly defined to begin with. Thus, in the above quotations, Sāṃkhya is obviously used in a variety of meanings. Properly speaking, a valid comparison is possible only between Classical Yoga and Classical Sāṃkhya in so far as both have the status of a philosophical *darśana*. And in this sense there can be no justification whatever for deriving Classical Yoga from Classical Sāṃkhya.

Recent research into the complex history of the Yoga and Sāṃkhya traditions has brought to light ample material to vindicate S. Dasgupta's (1930) conclusion that Patañjali's Yoga is a specific type of Sāṃkhya-Yoga just as the system of Classical Sāṃkhya is to be regarded as a separate line of development of the same common pool of ideas. As K. B. R. Rao (1966, 9) put it succinctly: 'We must guard against another obsession which has taken deep roots in our minds. It refers to the equation that is generally made of "atheistic Sāṃkhya" expounded in the *Sāṃkhya Kārikā*, with the one expounded in the *Yoga Sūtras* of Patañjali, with the exception of *īśvara* in the latter. It is an error of judgement to place the *Sāṃkhya Kārikā* and the *Yoga Sūtras*, or Kapila and Patañjali, in juxtaposition and treat them as preaching Atheism and Theism respectively [. . .] The *Yoga Sūtras* have Sāṃkhyan elements as Vedānta itself has, but its difference from the classical Sāṁkhya is as great as the difference between Vedānta and the classical Samkhya. The *Yoga-Sūtra-Sāṁkhya* is not simply classical Sāṃkhya plus God, nor the classical Sāṁkhya of the Sāṁkhya Kārikā is *Yoga-Sūtra-Sāṁkhya* minus God. They are fundamentally different in so many main principles.'

Now, the precise nature of these differences has never been ascertained in any appreciable detail. The reason for this is obvious: the absence of an unprejudiced study of the *Yoga-Sūtra* preceded by a critical appraisal of the exegetical literature. However, on the basis of the purged reading of the *Yoga-Sūtra*, rendered feasible by the present study, we are now in a position to re-examine these differences and undertake a comprehensive comparison between the *Yoga-Sūtra* and the *Sāṃkhya-Kārikā*. However, such a formidable task lies outside the compass of this investigation, and I must defer a detailed treatment of this promising line of research. For the present, I merely wish to point out the major divergencies between these two schools of thought as they have become apparent in the course of this study. I must emphasise at this point that I have certain misgivings about current interpretations of the *Sāṃkhya-Kārikā* as well. Hence before any exhaustive comparison could fruitfully be undertaken this text would also have to be examined both from a textual and a semantic point of view, so that we might arrive at a sterling understanding of this important scripture, unobscured (as far as this is possible) by all later interpretations and likely distortions. Until then one has to remain content with the rough identification of three areas of contrast between Classical Sāṃkhya and Pātañjala-Yoga, *viz.*

(1) methodology,
(2) doctrinal framework,
(3) terminology.

It is my contention that the different methodological approach of Classical Yoga is responsible for many of its conceptual and doctrinal as well as terminological idiosyncracies. I therefore commence this review with a brief examination of the methodological aspect. The importance of the distinct approach of Patañjali was pertinently emphasised by M. Eliade (1973[3], 7): '... whereas, according to Sāṃkhya, the only path to salvation is that of metaphysical knowledge, Yoga accords marked importance to techniques of meditation'. Elsewhere (p. 36) he remarked: 'Patañjali takes over the Sāṃkhya dialectic almost in its entirety, but he does not believe that metaphysical knowledge can, by itself, lead man to final liberation. Gnosis, in his view, only prepares the ground for the acquisition of freedom (*mukti*). Emancipation must, so to speak, be conquered by sheer force, specifically by means of an ascetic technique and a method of contemplation, which, taken together, constitute nothing less than the *yoga-darśana*.'

In a nutshell, whereas Classical Sāṃkhya relies heavily on the power of ratiocination and discernment, Classical Yoga, like any other yogic tradition, is founded on a philosophy which encourages personal experimentation and direct 'mystical' verification. This basic difference is anticipated in a well-known stanza in the *Mahābhārata* (XII.289.7): *pratyakṣa-hetavo yogāḥ sāṃkhyāḥ śāstra-viniścayāḥ, ubhe ca-ete mate tattve mama tata yudhiṣṭhira*, 'The Sāṃkhya-followers depend on [their] scriptures, [whilst] the Yoga-followers rely on direct-experience (*pratyakṣa*); both I deem [to convey] reality, friend Yudhiṣṭhira'. Even though on other occasions the unity of Yoga and Sāṃkhya is vigorously asserted, the above statement, which is by no means unique, clearly foreshadows the later bifurcation of both schools of thought into a 'rationalistic' and a 'mystical' system.

It is this experimental and experiential approach of Yoga,[3] as opposed to the more traditionalist Sāṃkhya, which can be regarded as the great stimulus underlying many of the doctrinal innovations leading to the creation of new schools within Hinduism as much as within Buddhism. The classical example of the seeker after truth who discards all theory in order to probe the depths of reality by means of his one-pointed mind is the founder of Buddhism himself. He first pursued his search with the help of existing 'models', of a Sāṃkhya and Yoga type, which he found of no avail. The Buddha then abandoned himself completely to a course of meditative exploration of his own device, which ultimately resulted in his *saṃbodhi* and in the formulation of one of India's most remarkable schools of thought.

The pronouncedly formalistic and rationalistic basis of Classical Sāṃkhya is readily borne out by the opening stanzas of the *Sāṃkhya-Kārikā*, which read: *duḥkha-traya-abhighātāj-jijñāsā tad-abhighātake hetau, dṛṣṭe sa-apārthā cen-na-eka-anta-atyantato'bhāvāt; dṛṣṭavad-anuśravikaḥ sa hy-aviśuddhi-kṣaya-atiśaya-yuktaḥ, tad-viparītaḥ śreyān-vyakta-avyakta-jña-vijñānāt*, 'Owing to the tribulation [stemming from the] threefold suffering [there arises] the desire-to-know the means of its removal. If [it be argued that] this [inquiry] is futile because visible [means of removal are available], [we reply that this is] not [the case], since [the visible remedies] are not final or abiding. – The revealed [cure for this tribulation] is like the visible [cure] [in the last analysis ineffective], for it is [also] connected with impurity, destruction and excess; different and superior to that is the discriminative-knowledge [by which is differentiated] the manifest, the unmanifest and the knower [*i.e.* the Self]'.

Thus the central expedient by which the termination of suffering (*duḥkha*) is effected is *vijñāna* or the careful holding apart of the three essential ontological categories postulated by Sāṃkhya. The technical terms *vyakta*, *avyakta* and *jña* are explained in the third stanza as (a) the evolutes of the world-ground, (b) the world-ground itself and (c) the *puruṣa*, and they are further defined in stanzas 10–11. In stanza 64, whose importance is generally overlooked, *vijñāna* occurs by the technical name of *tattva-abhyāsa* or the 'practice [affirming] the truth [as taught by Sāṃkhya]'. We are also told what this truth consists in. I cite the entire verse: *evaṃ tattva-abhyāsān-na-asmi na me na-aham-ity-apariśeṣam, aviparyayād-viśuddhaṃ kevalam-uipadyate jñānam*, 'Thus, on account of the practice of the truth [that] "I am not", "nothing is mine", "I am not" [there arises] [that] knowledge [which] is complete, pure and solitary because [it is] free from error'.

Tattva-abhyāsa, which is applied *vijñāna*, represents the effort to disrupt the habit of the empirical ego of identifying with the phenomenal contents of consciousness, so as to re-locate man's true identity in the transcendental Self. Man is essentially *puruṣa*, and in order to reach Self-authenticity he must divest himself of all phenomenal accretions, such as mind, body, external property or social relations.

That this intellectual distancing is not enough in itself is evident from the fact that Īśvara Kṛṣṇa also acknowledges the merit of moral purification (see 44). Moreover, as emerges from stanza 45, *vijñāna* must be accompanied by an act of renunciation of everything that reason – in keeping with tradition – has revealed to be 'non-self'. The verse in question reads: *vairāgyāt-prakṛti-layaḥ saṃsāro bhavati rajasād-ragāt* . . . , 'From dispassion [comes] the resolution [of the evolutes back into] the world-ground; from attachment [which is] passionate comes phenomenal-existence . . .'. Here *prakṛti-laya* does not, as in the *Yoga-Sūtra*, denote a sinking away into the world-ground by the human personality, but *laya* must be taken to refer to the dissolution of the evolutes coinciding with the recovery of the Self's authenticity. Any other reading would make no sense in the face of the fact that the avowed goal of Classical Sāṃkhya is the reinstalment of the Self in its untainted splendour of *kaivalya*. G. J. Larson's (1969) rendering of the phrase *vairāgyāt-prakṛti-layaḥ* as 'from non-attachment [comes] dissolution in *prakṛti*' is not explicit enough to avoid confusion with the peculiar usage of the term *prakṛti-laya* in Patañjali's work.

The sole interest of the follower of Classical Sāṃkhya is the disentanglement of *puruṣa* and *prakṛti*. This objective is shared not only by the antecedent Sāṃkhya-Yoga schools but also by Classical Yoga. Yet one cannot avoid the impression that the Sāṃkhya method of holding apart the primary categories of Self and non-self (= *prakṛti*) is executed on a level entirely different from that recommended by more meditation-oriented schools.[4] For, in the latter, the confusion between Self and mind (as a product of insentient nature), is held to be removable only by means of a controlled introversion and transformation of consciousness.

This does not appear to be the way of Classical Sāṃkhya. *Vijñāna* is by no means synonymous with *prajñā* or gnostic insight as acquired in *samādhi*; rather, it is an intellectual act of continuously reminding oneself that one is not this body, this particular sensation, feeling or thought. This is the famous *neti-neti* procedure of the upaniṣadic sages applied in the most rationalistic manner possible. In later Vedānta the same technique is known by the technical designation of *apavāda* or the 'annulment' of 'erroneous predication' (*adhyāropa*).[5] This intellectualistic refashioning of an originally introspective-meditative practice compelled J. N. Mukerji (1930, 8) to explain that 'the point of view of Sāṃkhya is logical and not psychological', which is probably a far too one-sided interpretation.

Furthermore, it is feasible that a perpetual distancing of oneself from the contents of consciousness might sooner or later induce altered states of awareness, nor is it entirely impossible that this was actually intended by Īśvara Kṛṣṇa and his disciples. The question is whether the approach of Classical Sāṃkhya is, in the last analysis, adequate for realising the postulated goal of Self authenticity. This is tacitly denied by the adherents of Yoga, who feel that the re-conditioning of the cognitive apparatus as achieved by the method recommended in Classical Sāṃkhya is not conducive to that complete rupture with the phenomenal which alone is capable of securing emancipation.

As the Yoga authorities are quick to point out, there are powerful traces in the depth-mind which no amount of rehabilitation will wipe out. These subliminal-activators (*saṃskāra*) must be rendered sterile by a restructuring of consciousness itself, which is brought about by disciplined introspection leading to *samādhi*. Hence, in Yoga, the Sāṃkhya *vijñāna* becomes *viveka-khyāti* or the gnostic vision of discernment. Similarly, *vairāgya* acquires a second dimension. On the ordinary level it is simply a letting go of externals, but in *samādhi* a second degree of detachment is called for which represents an act of will, subsequently leading to the much coveted *asaṃprajñāta-samādhi* in which all subliminal-activators become obliterated.

One may well speculate with K. B. R. Rao (1966, 432) that it is the accentuated rationalism of Classical Sāṃkhya which must be held responsible for the fact that this school of thought never actually acquired the same recognition and prestige as the other *darśanas*. Be that as it may, for the present purpose it is vital to realise that the methodological differences between Classical Sāṃkhya and Classical Yoga, as outlined above, initiated important conceptual and doctrinal divergencies which further increased the chasm between both schools of thought.

There are three major points in the doctrinal structure of Classical Yoga which mark it off from Classical Sāṃkhya, *viz*. theology, ontology and psychology. A fourth point occasionally suggested is the so-called *sphoṭa* doctrine which Patañjali is held to subscribe to, but as I will show, wrongly so.

The single most striking conceptual difference between both *darśanas* concerns their respective interpretation of, or attitude towards, theological reality. Whilst Classical Sāṃkhya is said to be *nir-īśvara* or 'atheistic', Classical Yoga (as apparently all forms of hindu Yoga) is most emphatically *sa-īśvara* or 'theistic'. This assertion is somewhat misleading. Although it is perfectly correct that Classical Yoga is intrinsically 'theistic', Classical Sāṃkhya cannot simply be styled 'atheistic'. The fact is that Īśvara Kṛṣṇa, rather like the Buddha, does not mention or make any statement about God at all. This can mean either of two things. He may deny outright the existence of such a supreme being, or else he may merely not lend any significance to this question or may postpone his judgement about it. In view of the absence of any positive denial of the existence of God and, considering the evidence of the late *Sāṃkhya-Sūtra*,[6] I would rather conjecture that Īśvara Kṛṣṇa assumed a typical agnostic stance. Ostensibly, if there be a God, he has little or nothing to do with the actual path of salvation as envisaged in Classical Sāṃkhya.

This indifference to theological matters is clearly out of tune with Classical Yoga, which is definitely theistic. As I have suggested above, against B. Heimann (1930, 90), there may possibly be an experiential basis for the concept of *īśvara*. However, I do not thereby wish to say anything affirmative about either the reality of the experience or the authenticity of the interpretations attached to it. If this stance is valid, the methodological factor can justly be said to be the cause of this most conspicuous difference between both *darśanas*.

The pre-eminently practical orientation of Yoga and its full reliance on first-hand evidence (*pratyakṣa*), rather than on traditional knowledge of a rationalistic slant is, moreover, responsible for subtle but nonetheless crucial divergencies in the ontological conceptions of the two systems. As I have tackled this question already, there is no need to repeat myself (see above pp. 112 ff.). Rather, what I am interested in at this point is the question of how to account for these differences. As I see it, the ontogenetic models were originally and primarily maps for meditative introspection, intended to guide the *yogin* in his exploration of the *terra incognita* of the mind. Thus these models served a very practical psychological purpose. This hypothesis helps to explain why so many of these models, as given out in the *Mahābhārata* and other early texts, are without apparent logical coherence. These 'maps' are records of internal experiences rather than purely theoretical constructions. They are descriptive rather than explanatory.

The 'map' character of the ontogenetic model of Classical Yoga is beyond question. The prakṛtic multi-level edifice is an eminently practical *ad hoc* conception which helps the *yogin* to 'program' his enstatic journey, to signpost his inward odyssey, so to speak, and to orientate himself properly so as not to depart from his original trajectory. Thus the levels of cosmogenetic evolution are simultaneously the levels of psychogenetic involution. Each subsequently 'deeper' layer within the prakṛtic organism becomes a target for the *yogin*'s conscious involutionary programme, until all levels of manifestation of the world-ground, and even the world-ground itself, are completely traversed. This is not a mere intellectual act.

The process of *samādhi* with its various degrees of completeness cannot be equated with the technique, utilised in Classical Sāṃkhya, of discriminating Self from non-self on the basis of prefabricated categories of differentiation. Yoga demands more than that. Overt conceptual discrimination or *vijñāna* is not enough. The categories of what represents the 'non-Self' must become the object of direct experience. The ultimate destination is of course the Self, as the experiencer behind all manifest contents of consciousness. In Classical Sāṃkhya, on the other hand, the ontogenetic model lacks this 'map' character and appears as a highly formalised structure typical of the rationalistic position of this school of thought.

The rigorous meditative-introspective discipline of Yoga, or, as J. W. Hauer (1958) put it, its 'experienced metaphysics' is furthermore responsible for the distinct holistic approach displayed by this tradition, which finds congenial expression in Patañjali's conception of mind. Whereas Īśvara Kṛṣṇa is mainly concerned with showing the various constituents of the inner world separately and in their evolutionary dependence, Patañjali emphasises the homogeneity of the human personality. This is clearly evinced by his concept of *citta*. Īśvara Kṛṣṇa's parallel term *liṅga* (or *karaṇa*),[7] used to denote the collectivity of the thirteen evolutes (*viz*. *buddhi*, *ahaṃkāra*, *manas* and the ten *indriyas*), is by no means synonymous with Patañjali's *citta*. It somehow lacks the unifying and integrating strength of the latter concept. Whereas *citta* is expressive of the dynamic interaction between the psychic structures – and thus is essentially a psychological concept – *liṅga* fails to convey any sense of dynamism or functional unity; it is primarily a static, analytical concept.

The last point adduced as a specific feature of the conceptual framework of Classical Yoga is the so-called *sphoṭa* doctrine.[8] This teaching, which originated among the early Sanskrit grammarians, contains the simple idea that a word is more than the sum total of its component letters. *Sphoṭa*, derived from √*sphuṭ* 'to burst open', is conceived as eternal and as manifesting itself in the spoken word. It represents the concept, brought to expression in a configuration of letters. Neither each separate sound nor the total sound of a word is considered as being capable of evoking a particular concept. Therefore, the *sphoṭa-vādins* conclude, there must be something more that inheres in a word which, when the word is heard, 'bursts forth' as meaning. On hearing the first sound we have a dark notion which becomes clearer as the word is uttered.

However, as E. Abegg (1914, 188 ff.)[9] has shown, *sphoṭa* has a strong metaphysical ingredient which is absent in our standard notion of 'concept', wherefore a straightforward equation of *sphoṭa* with 'concept' cannot be made. *Sphoṭa* is ultimately the plenum, *brahman*, and it is this aspect of the doctrine which was of cardinal importance to the Indians. As *brahman* is bodied forth in all contingent beings, so the concept of *brahman* is thought to be the root of all other concepts.

Now, if a definite reference to this recondite doctrine could be found in the *Yoga-Sūtra*, this would be a significant factor in support of the traditional claim that the author of the *Yoga-Sūtra* is identical with his namesake the grammarian. However, this does not seem to be the case. Patañjali himself nowhere mentions the word *sphoṭa*, and all later discussions about it are based on a single aphorism, namely III.17, which runs as follows: *śabda-artha-pratyayānām-itara-itara-adhyāsāt-saṃkaras-tat-pravibhāga-saṃyamāt sarva-bhūta-ruta-jñānam*, which may be rendered thus: 'Word, meaning and presented-idea of the corresponding object are [usually] present in a state of mixture because of their being each identified with each other. Through constraint (*saṃyama*) [on the distinction between] them, insight into the utterances of all beings is gained.'

As I understand it, this simply means that by nature *śabda*, *artha* and *pratyaya* are experienced as one. A sound uttered by a living being is always the bearer of meaning. It is also accompanied by an image in the mind of the percipient. If the sound is unknown, it can be understood by directly perceiving the idea in the mind of the sender. To achieve this direct perception or *sākṣātkāra* of the idea in the sender's consciousness, the *yogin* must make the distinction between word, meaning and image the subject of his meditative absorption and enstasy. This seems to be the plain message of the above *sūtra*.

There is no need here to assume that it contains any reference to *sphoṭa*. Considering the context in which it appears, it probably merely relates to the very practical matter of reading another person's mind, which is a generally recognised yogic feat. The explanations of Vācaspati Miśra and others must be rejected as too far-fetched. Interestingly, Vyāsa makes no mention of the term *sphoṭa* at all. According to him the matching of sounds with objects is purely conventional (*saṅketa*), and the act of recognising the meaning of words is a question of memory. Thus the blame for this whole confusion must be put on Vācaspati Miśra.

It is but natural that out of these methodological and conceptual divergencies there should also arise differences in the terminology adopted by Classical Yoga and Classical Sāṃkhya respectively. The preceding pages contain numerous examples which document this fact, and hence there is no need for duplication here. I merely wish to remind the reader of such specific yogic terms as *aliṅga*, *liṅga-mātra*, *asmitā-mātra*, *aviśeṣa*, *viśeṣa*, *citta*, *vṛtti* and *pratyaya* which are either absent in the *Sāṃkhya-Kārikā* or else have an entirely different connotation. The autonomy of the technical vocabulary of Classical Yoga is, I think, indisputable.

To sum up: as is apparent from a critical examination of the *Yoga-Sūtra*, far from being a mere imitation of Classical Sāṃkhya, Pātañjala-Yoga has all the characteristic marks of a thoroughly independent philosophical school of thought. Patañjali, or whoever may have been responsible for the composition of the *Yoga-Sūtra*, emerges as a striking personality who must be counted among the most creative minds of India. It would be almost frivolous to deny that he was intimately connected with the Yoga tradition and that he himself must have been a *yogin* of considerable attainment. He shows an unparalleled insight into yogic processes and, contrary to H. T. Colebrooke's (1873, I, 265) biased opinion, was not 'more mystic and fanatical' than Kapila, who 'makes a nearer approach to philosophical disquisition'. He had little sectarian inclination, if any. He showed a healthy respect for tradition, but not at the expense of the immediacy of personal verification. Far from burdening his epigones with unintelligible mumbo-jumbo, he produced a work of fine texture and remarkable insight which compares favourably with the philosophical creations of his contemporaries, and which has deservedly inspired countless generations of *yogins* of all denominations.

Notes

Chapter I

1 K. B. R. Rao (1966) follows one of the earlier editions of the *Mahābhārata* where this passage is XII.308.

2 P. M. Modi (1932, 62) wrongly contrasted this school with what he called 'rudrite' yoga. This entirely fictional yoga tradition arose as a misunderstanding of the phrase *rudra-pradhanān-aparān-viddhi yogān* (*Mahābhārata* XII.304.5[a]), where *rudra* clearly has the meaning of *prāṇa* ('breath'). See E. W. Hopkins (1901, 340). F. Edgerton (1965, 325), however, translates: 'know that there are other (inferior) Yoga-followers, of whom (the uncanny god) Rudra was the founder'.

3 See pp. 33 f. for an explanation of the terms *tamas* and *sattva*.

4 *Cf.* also *Bhagavad-Gītā* (VII.10): *bījaṃ māṃ sarva-bhūtānāṃ viddhi pārtha sanātanam*, 'know Me to be the external seed of all beings'. See also *Bhagavad-Gītā* X.39.

5 *Cf.* G. Oberhammer (1964, 197–207).

6 See *e.g.* *Nādabindu-Upaniṣad*.

7 *Cf.* S. Dasgupta's (1924, 163) position: 'It seems probable that Īśvara was traditionally believed in the Yoga school to be a protector of the Yogins [. . .] The metaphysical functions which are ascribed to Īśvara seem to be later additions . . .'

Chapter II

1 Of relevance here is F. S. C. Northrop's (1946, 447) discussion of 'Concepts of Postulation' *versus* 'Concepts of Intuition' and the critique by K. F. Leidecker (1954).

2 According to M. A. Mehendale (1960–61, 40), there is a further traditional etymology which is implied in the phrase *pumān retaḥ siñcati* . . . of *Muṇḍaka-Upaniṣad* (II.1.5), whereby the word *puruṣa* appears as a derivative of *pu* (*pumān*) + *ru* (*retas*) + *ṣa* (*siñcati*).

3 See *e.g.* *Ṛgveda* X.97.4–5.

4 See *e.g.* *Ṛgveda* X.90.3–4 and I.164.45, as also *Atharvaveda* II.1.2.

5 *Cf.* *Śatapatha-Brāhmaṇa* X.6.5.

6 See also the highly symbolic rites performed on the occasion of the installation of a temple, which is regarded as a manifestation of the *vāstu-*

puruṣa or supreme architect of the world. This is ably discussed in H. Zimmer (1926).

7 *Cf. Ṛgveda* III.62.10: *tat-savitur-vareṇyaṃ bhargo devasya dhīmahi dhiyo yo naḥ pracodayāt* (=*savitrī-mantra*).

8 See *e.g.* the *hiraṇyagarbha* tradition outlined in the *Mahābhārata* (XII.296.7[b]–8[a]), which says of the twenty-sixth principle that it is 'spotless, knowing, immeasurable, eternal; [yet] it apperceives always the twenty-fourth and the twenty-fifth' (. . . *vimalaṃ buddham-aprameyaṃ sanātanam, satataṃ pañca-viṃśaṃ ca catur-viṃśaṃ ca budhyate*). This invites comparison with the *Yoga-Sūtra* (IV.18), where the Self is described as continuously apperceiving the fluctuations of consciousness.

9 Even Patañjali (III.35) employs the term *bhoga*, without, however, meaning to ascribe any dynamics to the Self. *Bhoga* is 'experience', which is a consciousness event witnessed, or apperceived, by the Self.

10 *Cf. Yoga-Sūtra* IV.22, where *citi* is said to be *apratisaṃkramā*, which J. H. Woods (1966[3]) translates 'which unites not [with objects]'. As will be shown (pp. 53 f.), the co-operation between Self and consciousness is made possible by an apparent 'correlation' (*saṃyoga*), known to the epic teachers by the name of *miśratva* or 'association' (see *e.g. Mahābhārata* XII.295.21).

11 For a similarly loose and misleading use of language *cf.* G. J. Larson (1969, 183), who said about the Self that 'it is simply present in the world'.

12 G. J. Larson (1969) translated *pratiniyama* in a more conservative fashion as 'diversity'.

13 The commentators take the term *karaṇa* as referring to *buddhi*, etc.

14 The Sanskrit text reads . . . *ātmānaṃ bahudhā kṛtvā* . . ., 'making itself manifold'.

15 See *e.g. Muṇḍaka-Up.* I.2.9; *Śvetāśvatara-Up.* II.14.

Chapter III

1 See *e.g. Bhagavad-Gītā* III.27, 29, 33; IV.6; VII.5, 4, 20; IX.7, 8, 10, 12, 13; XI.51; XIII.19, 20, 23, 29; XVIII.59. *Śvetāśvatara-Upaniṣad* IV.10. *Maitrāyaṇīya-Upaniṣad* VI.10, 30; II.6. *Mahānārāyaṇa-Upaniṣad* X.8.

2 This strange relation between *Śvetāśvatara-Upaniṣad* and *Atharvaveda* is highlighted by the fact that IV.3 in the former scripture is a *verbatim* quotation from the latter, *viz.* X.8.27.

3 See *e.g. Bhagavad-Gītā* III.33, IV.6 *et al.*

4 See P. M. Modi (1932, 5) for a detailed study of the historical development of the *akṣara* concept.

5 This is what the post-Christian buddhist writers labelled *yogi-pratyakṣa*. As Th. Stcherbatsky (1958, 20–1) noted: 'Even the later Buddhist logicians, notwithstanding all their aversion to uncritical methods of thought, were nevertheless obliged to leave a loop-hole for the entrance of full mysticism and thus to support the religious theory of a Saint and of a Buddha. This loophole was a kind of intelligible intuition which was described as a gift to contemplate directly, as if present before the senses, that condition of the

Universe which, abstractly and vaguely, appeared as a necessary consequence of logic to the philosopher.'

6 See G. Feuerstein (1974, 87 f.).

7 See *Sāṃkhya-Kārikā* 22 and 24.

8 See W. Liebenthal (1934).

9 See E. Frauwallner (1953, 390).

10 See, for instance, F. Capra (1972, 15 ff.).

11 See the extensive bibliography of M. Eliade (1973[3]). Not mentioned but of paramount importance is the study by J. A. B. van Buitenen (1956–57) in the *Journal of the American Oriental Society*, vols. 76 (pp. 153 ff.) and 77 (pp. 15 ff. and 88 ff.). Also not listed are Th. Stcherbatsky (1934, 737–60) and A. Wayman (1962, 14–22).

12 J. A. B. van Buitenen (1956, 156).

13 See Vijñāna Bhikṣu's remarks to *Sāṃkhya-Sūtra* I.61: *sattva-ādīni dravyāṇi na vaiśeṣikā guṇāḥ*, '*sattva*, etc., are substances, not qualities [as taught in the school of] Vaiśeṣika'.

14 *Sāṃkhya-Kārikā* (11).

15 Vācaspati Miśra on *Sāṃkhya-Kārikā* (3); *cf. Sāṃkhya-Sūtra* (I.61): *sattva-rajas-tamasāṃ sāmya-avasthā prakṛtiḥ*.

16 See *Sāṃkhya-Kārikā* (12): *prīty-aprīti-viṣāda-ātmakāḥ prakāśa-pravṛtti-niyama-arthāḥ, anyo'nya-abhibhava-āśraya-janana-mithuna-vṛttayaś-ca guṇāḥ*, or 'The primary-constituents are embodied in pleasure, pain, indifference; [they] serve [the purposes of] manifestation–luminosity, activity and delimitation and have [as their] modes mutual domination, support, activation and interaction'.

17 G. M. Koelman's (1970, 78) coinage.

18 The term *prakāśa* (from *pra* + $\sqrt{}$*kāś* 'be visible, shine') has the dual connotation of 'manifestation' and 'luminosity'. The reason is not far to seek: the manifest universe is intimately bound up with radiation = light, a connection which did not escape the ancient sages.

19 See pp. 44 f.

20 See *Kaṭha-Upaniṣad* VI.8, *Maitrāyaṇīya-Upaniṣad* VI.31, 35; VII.2.

21 See *e.g.* Vācaspati Miśra's *Sāṃkhya-Tattva-Kaumudī* on *Sāṃkhya-Kārikā* 40 and Aniruddha's *Vṛtti* on *Sāṃkhya-Sūtra* VI.69. This native etymology was refuted by R. Garbe (1917[2], 328). See also E. A. Welden (1910, 445 f.).

22 This is R. E. Hume's (1931[2], 449) phrase (*ad Maitrāyaṇīya-Up.* VI.35).

23 See *e.g. Bṛhadāraṇyaka-Upaniṣad* IV.3.10 and *Chāndogya-Upaniṣad* II.24.16 and III.19.1. See also *Praśna-Upaniṣad* IV.8 and *Kauṣītaki-Upaniṣad* III.8. Similarly, *Bhagavad-Gītā* II.14 speaks of *mātrā-sparśāḥ* which can safely be translated as 'contacts with material-objects'. Śaṅkara, under the influence of Classical Sāṃkhya, misinterprets the word *mātrā* as *tanmātra*.

24 This was one of the mistakes committed by J. H. Woods (1966[3], 91), following Vācaspati Miśra, who (*ad* II.19) equates the *mahat-tattva* with *mahad-buddhi*.

25 S. Dasgupta (1963[5], I, 251).

26 According to another theory each *tanmātra* has but one character-

istic. See *Yuktidīpikā* on *Sāṃkhya-Kārikā* (25) *eka-uttaram-iti vārṣagaṇyaḥ*.

27 G. M. Koelman (1970, 107).

28 The Sanskrit text reads: *evaṃ tarhi na-eva-ahaṃkāro vidyata iti patañjaliḥ, mahato'smi-pratyaya-rūpatva-abhyupagamāt*, 'Thus then, there is no I-maker, [says] Patañjali, on account of the admission of the appearance of the notion of I-am in the great [entity]'. Of course, it is by no means settled that this Patañjali is identical with the *sūtra-kāra* or even that the words quoted by the author of the *Yuktidīpikā* are his *ipsissima verba*. P. Chakravarti (1951, 134 f.) has made a strong case against their identification, and conjectured that the Patañjali referred to in several passages of the aforementioned work is the same authority also cited by Padmapāda in his commentary on the *Prapañcasāra-Tantra* (I.94.7). We must also not forget that the *Yuktidīpikā* is, as A. Wezler (1974) has shown, a commentary on a commentary (the *Rāja-Varttika* quoted by Vācaspati Miśra in his *Sāṃkhya-Tattva-Kaumudī*, 72) and as such a comparatively late text.

29 S. Radhakrishnan (1951[6], II, 434).

30 This term makes its first appearance in the *Chāndogya-Upaniṣad* VII.25.1. This chapter, however, does not belong to the earliest parts of the text.

31 See *Tattva-Vaiśāradī* (II.19): *pañca tanmātrāṇi buddhi-kāraṇakāny-aviśeṣatvād-asmitāvad-iti*, 'the five potentials have *buddhi* as their cause because they are unparticularised, like I-am-ness'.

32 See *Sāṃkhya-Kārikā* (38): *tanmātrāṇy-aviśeṣaḥ tebhyo bhūtāni pañca pañcabhyaḥ, ete smṛtā viśeṣāḥ śāntā ghorāś-ca mūḍhāś-ca*, 'The potentials are unparticularised. From these five the five elements [originate]. These are held to be particularised tranquil, turbulent and delusive.'

33 G. J. Larson (1969), for one, seems oblivious to this whole argument. Interestingly, Umāsvāti, in his *Tattvārthādhigama-Sūtra* (II.16–18), distinguishes between *dravya-indriya* (the sense as substance) and *bhāva-indriya* (the sense as function). This Jaina work belongs, according to B. Bhatt (1977), to the second century A.D. and thus probably precedes Patañjali, who appears to have been aware of the doctrinal matter codified by Umāsvāti. *Cf. e.g.* YS II.30–31 with TS VII.1–2; YS I.33 with TS VII.6; YS I.21 (*saṃvega*) with TS VII.7; YS I.42–43 (*vitarka, vicāra*) with TS IX.41–46. H. Jacobi (1906), who translated this Prakrit text into German and noted some of these parallels with the *Yoga-Sūtra*, still placed Umāsvāti in the sixth century A.D. and consequently had to assume that the Jaina author utilised the *Yoga-Sūtra*, instead of *vice versa*.

34 It is not even clear whether this feat is thought to concern the *physical* body or its *subtle* counterpart (whose existence Patañjali may have denied).

Chapter IV

1 A. K. Lad (1967, preface).

2 This invites comparison with Plotinus' 'flight of the Alone to the Alone' (*Enneads* VI.9.11: φυγὴ μόνου πρὸς μόνον).

3 See J. A. B. van Buitenen's (1962) critical study.

4 A valuable beginning in this respect has been made by N. Tatia (1951).

5 *adṛṣṭo draṣṭā aśrutaḥ śrotā amato mantā avijñāto vijñātā na-anyo'to'sti draṣṭā na-anyo'to'sti śrotā na-anyo'to'sti mantā na-anyo'to'sti vijñātā eṣa ta ātma-antaryāmy-amṛtaḥ.*

6 See Vācaspati Miśra on aphorism I.4. Patañjali uses this word (II.53) and the cognate *yogyatva* (II.41) in a more general sense.

7 *Cf.* G. Kaviraj (1966, 128): 'The term "kaivalya" [. . .] conveys the sense of being "kevala" or alone. It implies the idea of purity and freedom from defilement.'

8 This imagery is peculiar to Vācaspati Miśra, who, in his gloss on II.20, states concisely: 'The casting of the Self's reflection into the mirror of *buddhi* [is the way in which] the Self can know the *buddhi*' (*buddhi-darpaṇe puruṣa-pratibimba-saṃkrāntir-eva buddhi-pratisaṃveditvaṃ puṃsaḥ*). For a detailed discussion of this reflection model see G. M. Koelman (1970, 48 f.).

9 As I have tried to show in a previous study (1979), the idiom of purity/purification is more particularly idiosyncratic of the *yoga-aṅga* section of the *Yoga-Sūtra* than of Patañjali's *kriyā-yoga* proper.

10 J. A. B. van Buitenen (1957b, 103).

11 See *Bhagavad-Gītā* VI.15; V.25, etc.

12 As the anonymous author of the *Sāṃkhya-Pravacana-Sūtra* (V.74–6) puts it pithily, 'Liberation is not the manifestation of bliss, for [the Self] has no qualities. – Nor, similarly, is it the destruction of particular qualities [inherent in the Self]. – Nor is it [any] particular movement of that motionless [Self]' (*na-ānanda-abhivyaktir-muktir-nirdharmatvāt, na viśeṣa-guṇa-ucchittis-tadvat, na viśeṣa-gatir-niṣkriyasya*).

Chapter V

1 See *e.g.* A. W. Watts (1961), H. Jacobs (1961) and G. Coster (1957⁶).

2 See *e.g.* R. Rösel (1928), P. V. Pathak (1931), S. Lindquist (1935), S. K. Saksena (1944), Swāmī Akhilānanda (1946) and E. Abegg (1955).

3 See *e.g.* *Ṛgveda* I.163.11; V.7.9; X.103.12, etc., and *Atharvaveda* I.34.2 (in the sense of 'intent' – a love spell).

4 But see *Chāndogya-Upaniṣad* VII.5.2, where the term appears in the following compounds: *cittavant, citta-ātman* and *citta-ekāyana*.

5 See *Sāṃkhya-Kārikā* 33 and Vācaspati Miśra's *Sāṃkhyatattva-kaumudī* thereon.

6 *Cf.* also T. R. Kulkarni (1972, 69): 'Patañjali clearly seems to have used the Sanskrit terms *citta* and *manas* interchangeably.'

7 This is a favourite simile with Sāṃkhya philosophers; see *e.g.* *Sāṃkhya-Pravacana-Bhāṣya* I.68; V.69, 91.

8 *yac-ca sva-bhāvaṃ pacati viśva-yoniḥ pācyāṃs-ca sarvān pariṇāmayed-yaḥ*, . . . 'The womb of all, which "cooks" [*i.e.* unfolds] its nature, and which transforms all "cookable-things" [*i.e.* evolved objects]'.

9 The word occurs twice in the locative (*pariṇāme*) and is usually trans-

lated by 'in the end'. This peculiar usage is also known to the *Aṣṭasāhasrikā* (VI.151).

10 See S. M. Katre (1968).

11 See *e.g.* *Sāṃkhya-Kārikā* 60, which describes the Self as 'unhelpful' (*anupakārin*).

12 See *Yoga-Bhāṣya* II.3.

13 I. K. Taimni (1965^2, 130).

14 The phrase 'seed of the defects' (*doṣa-bīja*) refers, of course, to the causes-of-affliction (*kleśa*), which must become, in Vyāsa's favourite metaphor, 'like burned seeds of rice', *dagdha-śāli-kalpāni*, III.50). *Cf.* *Mahābhārata* XII.204.16: *bījāny-agny-upadagdhāni na rohanti yathā punaḥ, jñāna-dagdhais-tathā kleśair-na-ātmā saṃbadhyate punaḥ*, 'Just as seeds roasted by fire do not germinate again, so also the Self is not bound by the causes-of-affliction burnt by gnosis'. *Cf.* also XII.179.15, which propounds what may be called a metaphysical 'germ theory': *bīja-mātraṃ purā sṛṣṭaṃ yad-etat-parivartate, mṛtā mṛtā praṇaśyanti bījād-bījaṃ pravartate*, 'It is only the seed, once discharged, which revolves; the dead are dead [and] gone; seed is produced from seed'.

15 The *Yoga-Bhāṣya* (IV.7) elucidates this thus: *catuṣpadā khalv-iyaṃ karma-jātiḥ, kṛṣṇā śukla-kṛṣṇā śuklā'śukla-akṛṣṇā ca-iti, tatra kṛṣṇā durātmanām, śukla-kṛṣṇā bahiḥ-sādhana-sādhyā, tatra para-pīḍā-anugraha-dvāreṇa-eva karma-āśaya-pracayaḥ, śuklā tapaḥ-svādhyāya-dhyānavatām, sā hi kevale manasy-āyatatvād-bahiḥ sādhana-anadhīnā na parān-pīḍayitvā bhavati, aśukla-akṛṣṇā saṃnyāsināṃ kṣīṇa-kleśānāṃ carama-dehānām-iti, tatra-aśuklaṃ yogina eva phala-saṃnyāsāt, akṛṣnaṃ ca-anupādanāt, itareṣāṃ tu bhūtānāṃ pūrvam-eva trividham-iti.* 'The class of *karman* is surely quadripartite: black, white/black, white and not-white/not-black. Of these the black [category] [pertains to] evil souls (*dur-ātman*); the white/black [category] is attainable by external means. The accumulation of action-deposit (*karma-āśaya*) of these [kinds of *karman*] is by way of [causing] harm (*pīḍā*) to or benefitting others. The white [category] [is peculiar to those who] practise austerities, self-study and meditation. Owing to the dependence of this [kind of *karman*] on the mind alone, it does not depend on external means and does not come about from injury to others. [That category which is] not-white/not-black [pertains to] the renunciants (*saṃnyāsin*) whose causes-of-affliction (*kleśa*) have dwindled [and who inhabit their] last bodies [never to be born again]. Of these [four kinds of *karman*] the not-white [category] [pertains to] the *yogin* owing to [his] renunciation of the fruit [of his actions] and the not-black [category] [is also peculiar to him alone] because of the exclusion (*an-upādāna*) [of such actions]. However, the triple [*karman*] [as explained] above, [is typical] of [all] other beings.'

16 *nirudhyante yasmin-pramāṇa-ādi-vṛttay'vasthā-viśeṣe cittasya so' vasthā-viśeṣo yogaḥ* (*Tattva-Vaiśāradi*, I.2).

17 See *e.g.* *Yoga-Bhāṣya* I.1: *sarva-vṛtti-nirodhe tv-asaṃprajñātaḥ samādhiḥ*, 'Upon the restriction of all the fluctuations, the ultra-cognitive enstasy [is achieved]'.

18 The Sanskrit commentators interpret the compound *viśeṣa-arthatva* as the 'particularity of an object'.

19 The Sanskrit text runs: *abhāva-pratyaya-ālambanā vṛttir-nidrā.*

20 As was pointed out by S. Pines and T. Gelblum (1966, 305), this

has been al-Bīrunī's understanding, or rather profound misunderstanding, of the compound. As the authors observed, he appears to have translated the *Yoga-Sūtra* relying 'to a considerable extent on his own intelligence and autodidactic capacity', that is to say, as an uninitiated outsider.

21 *Cf. Tattvārthādhigama-Sūtra* I.22, where the compound occurs as well: *bhava-pratyayo nāraka-devānām*, which is understood by the Jaina authorities to mean '[The supra-sensuous knowledge (avadhi)] of the hell-dwellers and the gods is congenital [lit. "birth-produced"]'. I have followed H. Jacobi's (1906) edition of the Śvetāmbara recension of this ancient Jaina text. In J. L. Jaini's (1920) edition of the Digambara recension (Vol. II of *Sacred Books of the Jainas*), this aphorism is numbered I.21, running *bhava-pratyayo-'vadhi* ... 'knowledge (*avadhi*) produced by birth ...'.

Chapter VI

1 One of the few scholars to have comprehended the full scope of these twin concepts was K. S. Joshi (1965), who wrote: 'This twofold process forms the very root of anything that claims to bear the name of "*yoga*"' (p. 60).

2 *Cf. Mahābhārata* XII.198.3–4: *sā-iyaṃ guṇavatī buddhir-guṇeṣv-eva-abhivartate, avatāra-abhiniḥsrotaṃ gireḥ śṛṅgād-iva-udakam; yadā nirguṇam-āpnoti dhyānaṃ manasi pūrvajam, tadā prajñāyate brahma nikaṣyaṃ nikaṣe yathā*. This can be translated as follows: 'The *buddhi*, endowed with the *guṇas*, extends only to the *guṇas*, flowing down-and-away [from the Self] like water from the peak of a mountain; [but] when it acquires the meditative-absorption devoid of the *guṇas* [and] born earlier on in the mind, then the Absolute (*brahman*) is verified, like a streak-of-gold on the touchstone.'

3 *Śrama* is frequently used already in the *Atharvaveda* (*e.g.* IV.35.2; VI.133.3; esp. XI.7.17 and XII.5.1).

4 G. Feuerstein (1974, 35).

5 Vācaspati explains the compound *eka-tattva* ('unitary principle') as referring to the 'lord' (*īśvara*). This is also al-Bīrūni's interpretation – a fact which seems to have eluded S. Pines and T. Gelblum (1966).

6 The aphorism runs: *virāma-pratyaya-abhyāsa-pūrvaḥ saṃskāra-śeṣo'nyaḥ*.

7 The earliest mention of this term is in the *Maitrāyaṇīya-Upaniṣad* (VI.18), but the underlying idea is clearly expressed already in the much older *Chāndogya-Upaniṣad* (VIII.15).

8 A familiar concept in the *Prajñāpāramitā* literature; see *e.g. Aṣṭa-Sāhasrikā* XI.240–41 and XXV.430.

9 See C. Albrecht (1951).

10 See A. Bharati's (1971, 261) appreciative remarks about this neologism ('a felicitous term created by Eliade to replace the cognitively inaccurate "ecstasy"').

11 *Cf. Mahābhārata* XII.287.12, *yathā bhānu-gataṃ tejo maṇiḥ śuddhaḥ samādhinā, ādatte rāja-śārdūla tathā yogaḥ pravartete*, 'As a pure jewel absorbs the solar glow, thus, o tiger among kings, is Yoga effected by enstasy'.

12 V. M. Bedekar (1960–61, 116 ff.) has drawn attention to an interest-

ing pre-classical exposition of *dhyāna-yoga* in the *Mahābhārata* (XII.188) in which the terms *vitarka* and *vicāra* make their appearance (stanza 15). They are described as phenomena of the first form or stage of meditative-absorption. A third factor is *viveka*, which V. M. Bedekar (p. 118) correctly understood as the 'disengaging the mind from the objects of sense'. However, in a subsequent publication (1968, 48) the author mistranslated this term as 'discrimination'. He also attempted to relate this fourfold Yoga, taught by Bhīṣma to Yudhiṣṭhira, to the buddhist teaching of the four *jhānas*, but entertained the view that both the epic and the buddhist sources probably drew from a common fount of yogic knowledge. For an exposition of the four *jhānas* (= *dhyāna*) see F. Heiler (1922², 43 ff.).

13 This Sanskrit text is highly elliptic and reads: ***prajñā-prāsādam-āruhya na-śocyāñ-śocato janān, jagatī-sthān-iva-adri-stho manda-buddhī-na-vekṣate.***

14 According to Vyāsa the word *tasya* refers to the *yogin* who has attained to the 'vision of discernment', but with Vijñāna Bhikṣu I prefer to relate it back to the compound *hāna-upāya* of II.26.

15 J. H. Woods's (1966³) index lists *viveka-jaṃ dhyānam* at III.52, which must be a slip, since his translation clearly presupposes °-*jñānam*.

16 See *Yoga-Bhāṣya* III.52.

17 R. Schmidt (1960, 124).

18 E. Conze (1962, 80) viewed the question of the origin of this fourfold practice differently: 'They are not specifically Buddhistic [. . .] and may have been borrowed from other Indian religious systems. For centuries they lay outside the core of the Buddhist effort, and the orthodox elite considered them as subordinate practices [but] in the Mahāyāna became sufficiently prominent to alter the entire structure of the doctrine . . .' Although the name would seem to betray the hindu origins of the set, nevertheless the earliest references to the four 'infinitudes' (Pāli: *appamaññā*) as they are also known, is not in hindu but in buddhist writings (*e.g.* concluding line of *Khuddakapāṭha* of the *Suttapiṭaka*).

19 E. Frauwallner (1953, I, 424) wrongly equated *prasaṃkhyāna* with *dhyāna*.

20 For some useful observations on the interpretation of the nature of this type of enstatic experience see J. Maréchal (1964², 186 ff.).

21 This substitution of *samādhi* by *dhyāna* is most unseasonable, but there can be no doubt that *dharma-megha-dhyāna* is in fact the same as *dharma-megha-samādhi*.

22 On the intrinsic complexity of the word *dharma* see E. Conze's (1962, 92 ff.) enlightening analysis.

23 M. Eliade (1973³, 84), for instance, retained the earlier interpretation: '. . . seems to refer to an abundance ("rain") of virtues that suddenly fill the yogin'.

24 See also *Saddharma-Puṇḍarīka* V.5, where the Buddha's teaching is compared to a great cloud shedding its refreshing load of water; *cf.* vss. 16 and 36 ff. See also XXIV.22. The ten stages were discussed in detail by N. Dutt (1930). See also H. Dayal (1932).

25 It is interesting to observe the interpretation of the concept of *dharma-megha-samādhi* in such Yoga-inspired Vedānta works as the *Paiṅgala-*

Upaniṣad (III.2) and the *Pañcadaśī* (I.60). The former text has this to say: *tato'bhyāsa-pāṭavāt-sahasraśaḥ sadā amṛta-dhārā varṣati, tato yoga-vittamāḥ samādhiṃ dharma-meghaṃ prāhuḥ*, 'Thence, through skill in practice, a stream of immortality/nectar showers forth always from thousand [directions]; therefore the most excellent knowers of Yoga call it the cloud of *dharma* enstasy'. This corresponds almost *verbatim* with the verse in Vidyāraṇya's popular exposition of Advaita-Vedānta: *dharma-megham-imaṃ prāhuḥ samādhiṃ yoga-vittamāḥ, varṣaty-eṣa yato dharma-amṛta-dhāraḥ sahasraśaḥ*, 'The most excellent knowers of Yoga call this enstasy "cloud of *dharma*" because it showers forth streams of *dharma* nectar by the thousands'.

26 M. Eliade (1973³, 86).

27 See my 1979 publication (pp. 74 ff.).

28 In this stanza *vibhūti* could possibly be used adjectivally; thus R. C. Zaehner (1969) translated 'far-flung' and took it to qualify the word *Yoga*.

29 T. Vidyāratna's (1914) edition, ch. I, p. 352.

30 *Sva-aṅga-jugupsā* is not so much disgust with one's body, as many translators would have it, but a healthy detachment towards it.

31 *Ātma-darśana* is explained in the *Mahābhārata* (XII.315.29) as follows: *ādarśe svām-iva chāyāṃ paśyasya-ātmānam-ātmanā* . . ., 'As one's image in a mirror [thus] you behold the Self by the Self'. Elsewhere (XII.196.4) we read: *na cakṣuṣā paśyati rūpam ātmano* . . ., 'The form of the Self cannot be seen by the eye'.

32 See my comments on p. 95.

33 See pp. 62 f.

34 However, according to J. Miller in G. Feuerstein and J. Miller (1971, 101) a possible parallel to the *kuṇḍalinī* conception may be found in certain usages of the multi-valent notion of fire (*agni*), as *e.g.* in *Ṛgveda* X.136.

Chapter VII

1 H. T. Colebrooke (1873, I).

2 *Op. cit.*, p. 265.

3 See *Mahābhārata* XII.294.7[a]: *yoga-kṛtyaṃ tu yogānāṃ dhyānam-eva paraṃ balam*, 'The superior strength of the Yoga-followers is [their practice of] meditative-absorption [of] Yoga praxis'.

4 This has its parallel in Buddhism in the relation between Asaṅga's Yogācāra and Nāgārjuna's intellectualist Mādhyamika.

5 See *e.g.* *Vedānta-Sāra* (33).

6 Unfortunately the date of this text is still problematic. Generally placed in the fourteenth or fifteenth century A.D., it undoubtedly contains much older material.

7 On the meaning of the term *liṅga* and its significance see R. Garbe (1894, 323 ff.). See also E. A. Welden (1914, 32–51).

8 See *e.g.* S. Dasgupta (1963⁵, I, 238, fn. 1): 'The most important point in favour of this identification [between the grammarian Patañjali and the author of the *Yoga Sūtra*] seems to be that both Patañjalis as against the

other Indian systems admitted the doctrine of *sphoṭa* which was denied even by Sāṃkhya.'

9 See also K. K. Raja (1956, 84–116).

Publications Cited

Abegg, E. (1914), 'Die Lehre vom Sphoṭa im Sarvadarśana-saṃgraha', in *Festschrift Ernst Windisch* (Leipzig), pp. 188 ff.

— (1955), *Indische Psychologie* (Zürich)

Albrecht, C. (1951), *Psychologie des mystischen Bewusstseins* (Bremen)

Bedekar, V. M. (1960–61), 'The Dhyānayoga in the Mahābhārata (XII.188)', *Munshi Indological Felicitation Volume, Bharatīya Vidyā*, XX–XXI, pp. 115–25

— (1968), 'Yoga in the Mokṣadharmaparvan of the Mahābhārata', *Beiträge zur Geistesgeschichte Indiens: Festschrift für E. Frauwallner* (Vienna), pp. 43–52

Bharati, A. (1970³), *The Tantric Tradition* (London)

— (1971), 'Anthropological Approaches to the Study of Religion: Ritual and Belief Systems', *Biennial Review of Anthropology*, pp. 230–81

Bhatt, B. (1977), 'Tattvārtha Studies III (Summary)', *Zeitschrift der dt. morgenländischen Gesellschaft*, Supplement III, 7, pp. 802–5

Bhattacharyya, K. (1956), *Studies in Philosophy*, vol. 1 (Calcutta)

Bowes, P. (1971), *Consciousness and Freedom* (London)

Buitenen, J. A. B. van (1956), 'Studies in Sāṃkhya I', *Journal of the American Oriental Society*, LXXVI, pp. 153 ff.

— (1957ᵃ), 'Studies in Sāṃkhya II', *op. cit.*, LXXVII, pp. 15 ff.

— (1957ᵇ), 'Studies in Samkhya III', *op. cit.*, LXXVII, pp. 88 ff.

— (1962), *The Maitrāyaṇīya-Upaniṣad* (The Hague)

Bulcke, C. (1947), *The Theism of the Nyāya-Vaiśeṣika* (Calcutta)

Burrow, T. (1948), 'Sanskrit *rájas*, *Bulletin of the School of Oriental and African Studies*, XII, pp. 645 ff.

Capra, F. (1972), 'The Dance of Shiva: the Hindu View of Matter in the Light of Modern Physics', *Main Currents in Modern Thought*, XXIX, pp. 15 ff.

Catalina, F. V. (1968), *A Study of the Self Concept of Sāṅkhya-Yoga Philosophy* (Delhi)

Chakravarti, P. (1951), *Origin and Development of the Sāṃkhya System of Thought* (Calcutta)

Chattopadhyaya, D. (1959), *Lokāyata* (New Delhi)

Colebrooke, H. T. (1873), *Miscellaneous Essays*, vol. 1 (London)

Conze, E. (1962), *Buddhist Thought in India* (London)

— (1967), *Thirty Years of Buddhist Studies* (London)

Coster, G. (1957⁶), *Yoga and Western Psychology: a Comparison* (London)

Dasgupta, S. (1920), *A Study of Patañjali* (Calcutta)

— (1924), *Yoga as Philosophy and Religion* (Calcutta) (1973²)

— (1930), *Yoga Philosophy in Relation to Other Systems of Indian Thought* (Calcutta)
— (1963[5]), *A History of Indian Philosophy*, vol. 1 (Cambridge)
— (1965[4]), *A History of Indian Philosophy*, vol. 2 (Cambridge)
Davids, C. A. F. Rhys (1936[3]), *The Birth of Indian Psychology and its Development in Buddhism* (London)
Dayal, H. (1932), *The Bodhisattva Doctrine in Buddhist Sanskrit Literature* (London)
Deussen, P. (1920[3]), *Allgemeine Geschichte der Philosophie*, vol. 1, pt. 3 (Leipzig)
Dutt, N. (1930), *Aspects of Mahāyāna Buddhism in its Relation to Hīnayāna* (London)
— (1934), *The Pañcaviṃśatisāhasrikā Prajñāpāramitā* (London)
Dvivedī, M. N. (1934[3]), *The Yoga-Sūtras of Patañjali* (Adyar)
Edgerton, F. (1924), 'The Meaning of Sāṅkhya and Yoga', *Journal of American Philology*, XLV, pp. 1 ff.
— (1965), *The Beginnings of Indian Philosophy* (London)
Eliade, M. (1973[3]), *Yoga: Immortality and Freedom* (Princeton)
— (1968[2]), *Myths, Dreams and Mysteries* (London)
Feuerstein, G., and Miller, J. (1971), *A Reappraisal of Yoga* (London)
Feuerstein, G. (1974), *The Essence of Yoga* (London)
— (1979), *The Yoga-Sūtra of Patañjali: an Exercise in the Methodology of Textual Analysis* (New Delhi)
Flagg, W. J. (1898), *Yoga or Transformation* (New York and London)
Frauwallner, E. (1953), *Geschichte der indischen Philosophie*, vol. 1 (Salzburg)
Garbe, R. (1894), *Sāṃkhya und Yoga* (Strassburg)
— (1899), *Sāṃkhya-Pravacana-Bhāṣya* (Leipzig)
— (1917[2]), *Die Sāṃkhya-Philosophie* (Leipzig)
Ghosh, J. (1934), *The Sāṃkhya Sūtras of Pañcaśikha and Other Ancient Sages* (Chinsura)
Gonda, J. (1960), *Die Religionen Indiens*, vol. 1 (Stuttgart)
Goswāmi Dāmodara Śāstri (1935), *Saṅgayogadarśana* (Benares)
Goswāmī, D. L. (1903), *Pātañjaladarśana* (Benares)
Hauer, J. W. (1922), *Die Anfänge der Yogapraxis* (Stuttgart)
— (1927), *Das Laṅkāvatāra-Sūtra und das Sāṃkhya* (Stuttgart)
— (1931), 'Das IV. Buch des Yogasūtra', in *Ehrengabe für Wilhelm Geiger*, ed. W. Wüst (Leipzig), pp. 122 ff.
— (1958), *Der Yoga* (Stuttgart)
Heiler, F. (1922[2]), *Die buddhistische Versenkung* (Munich)
Heimann, B. (1930), *Studien zur Eigenart indischen Denkens* (Tübingen)
Hill, W. D. P. (1966[2]), *The Bhagavadgītā* (London) [1928[1]]
Hopkins, E. W. (1901), 'Yoga-technique in the Great Epic', *Journal of the American Oriental Society*, XXII, 333–79.
Hultzsch, E. (1927), 'Sāṃkhya und Yoga im Śiśupālavadha', *Aus Indiens Kultur: Festgabe für Richard von Garbe*, ed. J. von Negelein (Erlangen), pp. 78 ff.
Hume, R. E. (1931[2]), *The Thirteen Principal Upanishads* (London) [1958[4]]
Jacob, G. A. (1891), *A Concordance to the Principal Upanishads and Bhagavadgītā* (Bombay)

Jacobi, H. (1906), 'Eine Jaina Dogmatik', *Zeitschrift der morgenländischen Gesellschaft*, LX, pp. 287–325 and 512–51
— (1923), *Die Entwicklung der Gottesidee bei den Indern* (Bonn and Leipzig)
— (1929), 'Über das ursprüngliche Yoga-System', *Sitzungsberichte der Preussischen Akademie der Wissenschaften* (Berlin), pp. 581 ff.
Jacobs, H. (1961), *Western Psychotherapy and Hindu Sādhanā* (London)
Janáček, A. (1951), 'The methodological principle in Yoga', *Archiv Orientální*, XIX, pp. 514–67
— (1954), 'The "voluntaristic" type of Yoga in Patañjali's Yoga-Sūtras', *Archiv Orientální*, XXII, pp. 70 ff.
— (1957), 'The meaning of pratyaya', *Archiv Orientální*, XXV, pp. 201–60
— (1958), 'Two texts of Patañjali and a statistical comparison of their vocabularies', *Archiv Orientální*, XXVI, pp. 88 ff.
Jaini, J. L. (1920), *Tattvarthadhigama Sutra* (Arrah)
Jennings, J. G. (1947), *The Vedāntic Buddhism of the Buddha* (London)
Jha, G. (1907), *The Yoga-Darśana* (Bombay)
— (1933²), *Yoga-Sāra-Saṃgraha* (Adyar)
Johnston, Ch. (1964), *The Yoga Sutras of Patañjali* (London)
Johnston, E. H. (1937), *Early Sāṃkhya* (London)
Joshi, K. S. (1965), 'On the Meaning of Yoga', *Philosophy East and West*, XV, 1, pp. 53–64
Kane, P. V. (1962), *History of Dharmaśāstra*, vol. V, pt. 2 (Poona)
Katre, S. M. (1968), *Dictionary of Pāṇini*, vol. 2 (Poona)
Kaviraj, G. (1966), *Aspects of Indian Thought* (Burdwan)
Kenghe, C. T. (1958), 'The Concept of Prakṛti in the Sāṃkhya Philosophy', *Poona Orientalist*, XXIII, pp. 1 ff.
Kielhorn, F. (ed.) (1892²), *Vyākarana-Mahābhāṣya of Patañjali*, vol. 1 (Bombay)
Koelman, G. M. (1970), *Pātañjala Yoga* (Poona)
Krishnamacharya, E. (1931), *Jayakhyasaṃhitā* (Baroda)
Kuhn, T. S. (1970²), *The Structure of Scientific Revolutions* (Chicago)
Kulkarni, T. R. (1972), *Upanishads and Yoga* (Bombay)
Kumarappa, B. (1934), *The Hindu Conception of the Deity* (London)
Kunst, A. (1968), 'Somatism: a Basic Concept in India's Philosophical Speculations', *Philosophy East and West*, XVIII, 4, pp. 261–75
Kunz, F. L. (1963), *The Reality of the Non-Material* (Mount Vernon)
Lad, A. K. (1967), *A Comparative Study of the Concept of Liberation in Indian Philosophy* (Burhanpur)
Larson, G. J. (1969), *Classical Sāṃkhya* (Delhi)
Laski, M. (1965²), *Ecstasy: a Study of Some Secular and Religious Experiences* (London)
Lauenstein, D. (1943), *Das Erwachen der Gottesmystik in Indien* (Munich)
La Vallée Poussin, L. de (1936–37), 'Le Bouddhisme et le Yoga de Patañjali', *Mélanges chinois et bouddhiques*, V, pp. 223 ff.
Leidecker, K. F. (1954), 'Concepts of Intuition and the Nature of Sanskrit Philosophical Terminology', *Philosophical and Phenomenological Analysis*, XV, 4, pp. 230–7
Leumann, E. (n.d.), *Zeitschrift für Sprachforschung*, XXXII, pp. 10 ff.

Liebenthal, W. (1934), *Satkāryavāda in der Darstellung seiner buddhistischen Gegner* (Stuttgart and Berlin)
Lindquist, S. (1935), *Die Methoden des Yoga* (Lund)
Mackie, J. (1947), 'Scientific Method in Textual Criticism', *Australasian Journal of Psychology and Philosophy*, XV, pp. 53 ff.
Mahadeva Sastri, A. M. (1968²), *Yoga Upanisads with the Commentary of Śrī Brahma-Yogin* (Adyar)
Majumdar, A. K. (1968), 'Theism in Indian Religions', *Bharatiya Vidya*, XXVIII
Maréchal, J. (1964²), *Studies in the Psychology of the Mystics* (Albany, N.Y.)
Mashruwala, K. G. (1950), 'Guru Cult', *Indian Philosophical Congress Silver Jubilee Commemoration Volume* (Basavanagudi), pp. 237–45
Mehendale, M. A. (1960–61), 'Upanisadic Etymologies', *Munshi Indological Felicitation Volume Bharatīya Vidyā*, XX–XXI, pp. 40–4
Mitra, R. (1883), *The Yoga Aphorisms of Patañjali* (Calcutta)
Modi, P. M. (1932), *Akṣara* (Baroda)
Monier-Williams, M. (1894), *Hinduism* (London)
Müller, M. (1916⁴), *The Six Systems of Indian Philosophy* (London)
Mukerji, J. N. (1930), *Sāṁkhya or the Theory of Reality* (Calcutta)
Myrdal, G. (1973), 'The Beam in our Eye', *Comparative Research Methods*, ed. D. P. Warwick and S. Osherson (Englewood Cliffs, N.J.), pp. 89 ff.
Northrop, F. S. C. (1946), *The Meeting of East and West* (New York)
Oberhammer, G. (1964), 'Gott, Urbild der emanzipierten Existenz im Yoga des Patañjali', *Zeitschrift für Katholische Theologie*, pp. 197 ff.
— (1965), 'Meditation und Mystik im Yoga des Patañjali', *Wiener Zeitschrift für die Kunde Süd- und Ostasiens*, IX, pp. 98 ff.
Oldenberg, H. (1915), *Die Lehre der Upanishaden und die Anfänge des Buddhismus* (Göttingen)
Otto, R. (1959), *The Idea of the Holy* (Harmondsworth)
Pathak, P. V. (1931), *The Heyapaksha of Yoga, or Towards a Constructive Synthesis of Psychological Material in Indian Philosophy* (Ahmedabad)
Pandeya, R. C. (1967), *Yuktidīpikā* (Delhi)
Pensa, C. (1969), 'On the Purification Concept in Indian Tradition, with special regard to Yoga', *East and West* (n.s.) XIX, pp. 1–35
— (1973ᵃ), 'Observations and References for the Study of Ṣaḍaṅgayoga', *Yoga Quarterly Review*, IV, pp. 9 ff.
— (1973ᵇ), 'The Powers (Siddhis) in Yoga', *Yoga Quarterly Review*, V, 9 ff.
Pines, S., and Gelblum, T. (1966), 'Al-Bīrūnī's Arabic Version of Patañjali's *Yoga-Sūtra*', *Bulletin of the School of Oriental and African Studies*, XXIX, pp. 302–25
Prasāda, R. (1912), *Patanjali's Yoga Sutras* (Allahabad)
Radhakrishnan, S. (1927), *Hindu Mysticism* (Chicago and London)
— (1951⁶), *Indian Philosophy*, vol. 1 (London)
— (1960), *The Brahma Sūtra* (London)
Raja, K. K. (1956), 'Sphoṭa: the Theory of Linguistic Symbols', *Adyar Library Bulletin*, XX, pp. 84 ff.
Rao, K. B. R. (1966), *Theism of Preclassical Sāmkhya* (Prasaranga)
Rösel, R. (1928), *Die psychologischen Grundlagen der Yogapraxis* (Stuttgart)

Sahay, M. (1964), 'Pātañjalayogasūtras and the Vyāsa Bhāṣya', *Vishveshvaranand Indological Journal*, II, pp. 254 ff.
Saksena, S. K. (1944), *Nature of Consciousness in Hindu Philosophy* (Benares)
Schmidt, R. (1960), *Immanuel Kant – Die drei Kritiken* (Stuttgart)
Schrader, F. O. (1916), *Introduction to the Pāñcarātra and the Ahirbudhnya Saṃhitā* (Adyar)
— (1955), 'Sāṃkhya Original and Classical', *Adyar Library Bulletin*, XIX, pp. 1–2
Schroeder, L. von (1887), *Indiens Literatur und Cultur* (Leipzig)
Seal, B. N. (1915), *The Positive Sciences of the Ancient Hindus* (London)
Senart, É. (1915), '*Rajas* et la théorie indienne des trois *guṇa*', *Journal asiatique*, XI, pp. 151 ff.
— (1925), 'La Théorie des *guṇas* et la *Chāndogya Upaniṣad*', *Études asiatiques*, II, pp. 285 ff.
Sharma, C. (1960), *A Critical Survey of Indian Philosophy* (London)
Shastri, D. N. (1976²), *The Philosophy of Nyāya-Vaiśeṣika and its Conflict with the Buddhist Dignāga School* (Varanasi)
Shree Purohit Swami (1938), *Aphorisms of Yoga* (London)
Sinari, R. A. (1970), *The Structure of Indian Thought* (Springfield, N.J.)
Singh, L. A. (1970), *Yoga Psychology: Methods and Approaches* (Varanasi)
Śivanārāyaṇa Śāstri (1940), *Sāṃkhyakārikā* (Bombay)
Smart, N. (1964), *Doctrine and Argument in Indian Philosophy* (London)
— (1968), *The Yogi and the Devotee* (London)
— (1971), *The Religious Experience of Mankind* (London and Glasgow)
Snellgrove, D. L. (1959), *The Hevajra Tantra*, vol. 1 (London)
Sokolov, E. N. (1963), *Perception and the Conditioned Reflex* (Oxford)
Stcherbatsky, T., and Obermiller, E. (1929), *Abhisamāyalaṅkāra-Prajñāpāramitā-Upadeśa-Śāstra* (Leningrad)
Stcherbatsky, T. (1934), 'The "Dharmas" of the Buddhists and the "Guṇas" of the Sāṃkhyas', *Indian Historical Quarterly*, pp. 737 ff.
— (1958), *Buddhist Logic*, vol. 1 ('s-Gravenhage)
Suryanarayana Sastri, S. S., and Raja, C. K. (1933), *The Bhāmatī of Vācaspati* (Adyar)
Swāmī Akhilānanda (1946), *Hindu Psychology* (New York)
Taimni, I. K. (1965²), *The Science of Yoga* (Adyar)
Takagi, S. (1966), 'On the "Kriyā-Yoga" in the Yoga-Sūtra', *Journal of Indian and Buddhist Studies*, XV, 24 ff.
Tatia, N. (1951), *Studies in Jaina Philosophy* (Benares)
Tuxen, P. (1911), *Yoga* (Copenhagen)
Upadhyaya, K. N. (1971), *Early Buddhism and the Bhagavadgītā* (Delhi)
Vidyāratna, T. (1914), *Prapañcasāra-Vivaraṇavyākhyā* (Calcutta and London)
Watts, A. W. (1961), *Psychotherapy East and West* (New York)
Wayman, A. (1962), 'Buddhist Dependent Origination and the Sāṃkhya Guṇas', *Ethnos*, pp. 14 ff.
Welden, E. A. (1910), 'The Sāṃkhya Term Liṅga', *American Journal of Philology*, XXXI, pp. 445–59
— (1914), 'The Sāṃkhya Teachings in the Māitrī Upaniṣad', *American Journal of Philology*, XXXV, pp. 32 ff.

Weller, F. (1953), *Versuch einer Kritik der Kathopaniṣad* (Berlin)
Wezler, A. (1974), 'Some Observations on the Yuktīdipikā', *Zeitschrift der dt. morgenländischen Gesellschaft*, Supplement II (vol. XVIII), pp. 434–55
Whatmough, J. (1954), 'Statistics and Semantics', *Sprachgeschichte und Wortbedeutung: Festschrift Albert Debrunner* (Berne), pp. 441 ff.
Whitehead, A. N. (1938[8]), *Science and the Modern World* (Harmondsworth)
Winternitz, M. (1922), *Geschichte der indischen Litteratur*, vol. 3 (Leipzig)
Wogihara, U. (ed.) (1908), *Asaṅga's Bodhisattva-bhūmi* (Leipzig)
Woods, J. H. (1915), 'The Yoga-sūtras of Patañjali as Illustrated by the Commentary entitled The Jewel's Lustre or Maṇiprabhā', *Journal of the American Oriental Society*, XXXIV, pp. 1 ff.
— (1966[3]), *The Yoga-System of Patañjali* (Delhi)
Zaehner, R. C. (1969), *The Bhagavad-Gītā* (Oxford)
Zigmund-Cerbu, A. (1963), 'The Ṣaḍaṅgayoga', *History of Religions*, III, pp. 128 ff.
Zimmer, H. (1926), *Kunstform und Yoga im indischen Weltbild* (Berlin)
— (1953[2]), *Philosophies of India* (London)

Index